TOAST
OF THE
TOWN

TOAST
OF THE
TOWN

◆

The Life and Times
of Sunnie Wilson

Sunnie Wilson with
John Cohassey

Wayne State University Press   Detroit

Great Lakes Books

*A complete listing of the books in this series
can be found at the back of this volume.*

Philip P. Mason, Editor
Department of History, Wayne State University

Dr. Charles K. Hyde, Associate Editor
Department of History, Wayne State University

02 01 00 99 98   5 4 3 2 1

Library of Congress Cataloging-in-Publication Data

Wilson, Sunnie, 1908–
    Toast of the town : the life and times of Sunnie Wilson / Sunnie
Wilson with John Cohassey.
        p.   cm. — (Great Lakes books)
    ISBN 0-8143-2695-1 (alk. paper)
    1. Wilson, Sunnie, 1908–   . 2. Hotelkeepers—Michigan—Detroit—
Biography.   3. Louis, Joe, 1914–   . 4. Afro-American
businesspeople—Michigan—Detroit.   5. Detroit (Mich.)—History.
I. Cohassey, John, 1961–   . II. Title. III. Series.
TX910.5.W58A3   1998
647.94¢092—dc21
[B]   97-25475

About the endpapers: Two views of the Forest Club, which Sunnie Wilson
owned from 1941 to 1951. The exterior view shows the Club at the corner of
Forest and Hastings. The interior view highlights the 107-foot bar, the "longest
bar in town."

Dedicated with love to my grandchildren,
Burton, Brooke, and Brigette,
to my great-grandchildren,
Christopher, Bailey, and Nicholas,
and to Margaret Samples,
whose warmth and companionship
have brightened my years

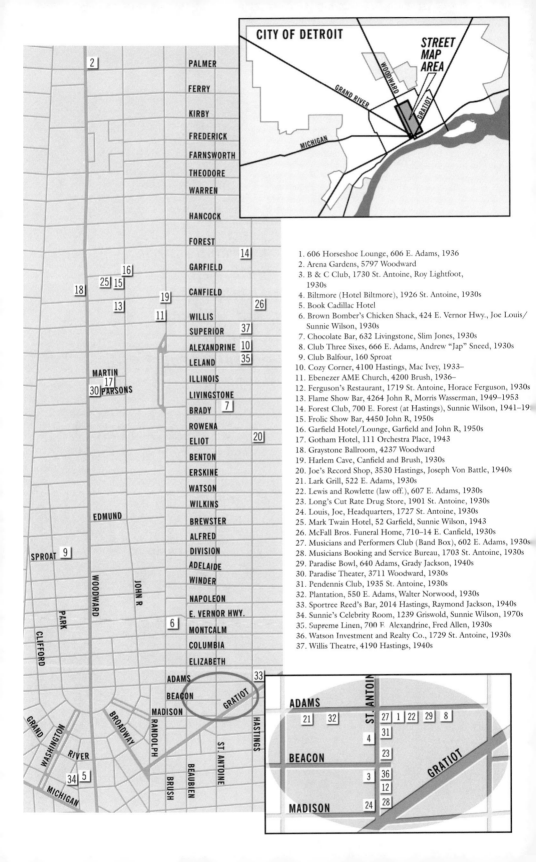

CITY OF DETROIT

STREET MAP AREA

WOODWARD
GRAND RIVER
GRATIOT
MICHIGAN

PALMER
FERRY
KIRBY
FREDERICK
FARNSWORTH
THEODORE
WARREN
HANCOCK
FOREST
GARFIELD
CANFIELD
WILLIS
SUPERIOR
ALEXANDRINE
LELAND
ILLINOIS
LIVINGSTONE
BRADY
ROWENA
ELIOT
BENTON
ERSKINE
WATSON
WILKINS
BREWSTER
ALFRED
DIVISION
ADELAIDE
WINDER
NAPOLEON
E. VERNOR HWY.
MONTCALM
COLUMBIA
ELIZABETH
ADAMS
BEACON
MADISON
GRATIOT

MARTIN
PARSONS
EDMUND
SPROAT
WOODWARD
JOHN R
PARK
CLIFFORD
GRAND RIVER
WASHINGTON
MICHIGAN
BROADWAY
RANDOLPH
BEAUBIEN
BRUSH
ST. ANTOINE
HASTINGS

ADAMS
BEACON
MADISON
ST. ANTOINE
GRATIOT

1. 606 Horseshoe Lounge, 606 E. Adams, 1936
2. Arena Gardens, 5797 Woodward
3. B & C Club, 1730 St. Antoine, Roy Lightfoot, 1930s
4. Biltmore (Hotel Biltmore), 1926 St. Antoine, 1930s
5. Book Cadillac Hotel
6. Brown Bomber's Chicken Shack, 424 E. Vernor Hwy., Joe Louis/ Sunnie Wilson, 1930s
7. Chocolate Bar, 632 Livingstone, Slim Jones, 1930s
8. Club Three Sixes, 666 E. Adams, Andrew "Jap" Sneed, 1930s
9. Club Balfour, 160 Sproat
10. Cozy Corner, 4100 Hastings, Mac Ivey, 1933–
11. Ebenezer AME Church, 4200 Brush, 1936–
12. Ferguson's Restaurant, 1719 St. Antoine, Horace Ferguson, 1930s
13. Flame Show Bar, 4264 John R, Morris Wasserman, 1949–1953
14. Forest Club, 700 E. Forest (at Hastings), Sunnie Wilson, 1941–19
15. Frolic Show Bar, 4450 John R, 1950s
16. Garfield Hotel/Lounge, Garfield and John R, 1950s
17. Gotham Hotel, 111 Orchestra Place, 1943
18. Graystone Ballroom, 4237 Woodward
19. Harlem Cave, Canfield and Brush, 1930s
20. Joe's Record Shop, 3530 Hastings, Joseph Von Battle, 1940s
21. Lark Grill, 522 E. Adams, 1930s
22. Lewis and Rowlette (law off.), 607 E. Adams, 1930s
23. Long's Cut Rate Drug Store, 1901 St. Antoine, 1930s
24. Louis, Joe, Headquarters, 1727 St. Antoine, 1930s
25. Mark Twain Hotel, 52 Garfield, Sunnie Wilson, 1943
26. McFall Bros. Funeral Home, 710–14 E. Canfield, 1930s
27. Musicians and Performers Club (Band Box), 602 E. Adams, 1930s
28. Musicians Booking and Service Bureau, 1703 St. Antoine, 1930s
29. Paradise Bowl, 640 Adams, Grady Jackson, 1940s
30. Paradise Theater, 3711 Woodward, 1930s
31. Pendennis Club, 1935 St. Antoine, 1930s
32. Plantation, 550 E. Adams, Walter Norwood, 1930s
33. Sportree Reed's Bar, 2014 Hastings, Raymond Jackson, 1940s
34. Sunnie's Celebrity Room, 1239 Griswold, Sunnie Wilson, 1970s
35. Supreme Linen, 700 E. Alexandrine, Fred Allen, 1930s
36. Watson Investment and Realty Co., 1729 St. Antoine, 1930s
37. Willis Theatre, 4190 Hastings, 1940s

Contents

Acknowledgments and Author's Note

First and foremost, Mr. Wilson would like to express his regrets to the numerous individuals whom, due to the limitations of writing time and length of this work, he did not include in his memoir. Mr. Wilson and I express our appreciation to those whose time and effort contributed to the completion of the book. Much thanks must be extended to Detroit political consultant Adolph Mongo, who introduced me to Mr. Wilson and made possible the writing of a historically important memoir and lasting friendship. Our editor, and my close friend, Professor Roy Kotynek, proved invaluable in his direction and initial reading of the manuscript. In the area of photography and art direction we are grateful for the contributions of Michael T. Paradise and Darien Nemer, both of whom went far beyond our expectations. Mr. Wilson's daughter and son-in-law, Sharon and Burton Cardwell, have provided much assistance as well.

Thanks must be given to Detroiters Gus Adams, Johnnie Bassett, Alberta Adams, Carl Hill, and Jackie McLeod. We thank the staff of the Detroit Public Library's Burton Historical Collection, most notably David Poremba, whose assistance proved very helpful in the acquisition of archival photographs. Our appreciation also goes out to members of the Charter Township of Shelby Historical Committee and Idlewild's Inspector Norm Burns. My personal debt is to my wife, Gretta Abu-Isa, a patient companion and a wellspring of support.

Preface
Detroit's Most Congenial Host

Dressed in his trademark red hat, brightly colored suits, and Ellington-string tie, Sunnie Wilson is a combination of class and character, an ambassador of goodwill who has befriended many of the twentieth-century's most talented and powerful figures. For decades he sought to make his businesses places of refinement for black Detroiters. Opposed to the poor conditions of most segregated "colored hotels," he opened a sixty-two-room hotel to accommodate black travelers and musicians denied access to white establishments. As he stated, "I've always tried to protect my black folks because when I would travel I would get rooms infested with roaches and mice."

Over the years he provided musicians with hotel accommodations and monetary loans—philanthropic contributions that have earned him a national reputation as a impresario of African American music. Looking back over his past with its countless cast of characters and settings, Mr. Wilson lays claim to a life rich in human friendship. "You name 'em and I claim 'em," he says, referring to the celebrities he has known. He reminds those listening, "I don't need any history book on this city's black folks because I was there."

At our first meeting in a downtown Detroit restaurant, Sunnie Wilson took out an old black-and-white photograph. "That's my friend, Mr. Joe Louis," he announced, pointing to a picture

11

that revealed a somber, baby-faced Joe Louis and a young Sunnie Wilson. "My greatest and most humble friend," Mr. Wilson said with a sense of pride. After a few moments of study, I realized Mr. Wilson's expression in the photograph bore a remarkable likeness to the warm smile on Mr. Wilson's face, as if time had forgotten the fifty years since he stood next to the 1937 heavyweight champion of the world.

Soon I began to discover the qualities of a man known to local and national celebrities as "Detroit's most congenial host." Until our introduction, I knew Mr. Wilson only through newspaper articles, books, and the conversations of Detroiters who, upon learning about my study of the city's legendary Hastings Street, urged me to contact the man most connected with that historical street. Over time, Mr. Wilson and I became partners, a term he applies to a shared human endeavor based upon mutual trust rather than a monetary arrangement.

During the first months of our association, I was struck by Mr. Wilson's rapport with his fellow Detroiters. Driving downtown with him amid the noise of traffic, I heard shouts of "Sunnie!" as we passed the waving hands of well-dressed businessmen, delivery people, and passers-by. Over store counters old friends announced his presence with the familiar introduction, "Sunnie Wilson, Forest Club, Forest and Hastings!"

In his eighty-ninth year Mr. Wilson retains a vibrant spirit and a deep moral belief in the advancement of humanitarian principles. His genuine concern for the progress of young African Americans prompted him to do this book. In an age when many Americans view the past with a sense of disillusionment, Mr. Wilson offers a look into the lives of people who struggled to establish careers in business, politics, and entertainment. He reveals the entrepreneurial spirit of early black business pioneers and the lessons taught by their incessant determination to overcome segregation and economic depression in order to establish careers, homes, and organizations that fostered the progress of their people. Mr. Wilson hopes to inspire younger individuals to resume the pursuit of self-reliance, education, and racial pride built upon the creation of black-owned businesses and financial enterprises.

This work is not the story of one man, but one man's story centered around the lives of those who struggled to build a Detroit community. Mr. Wilson has given us a vital source with which to assess and reflect upon the past as we enter the twenty-first century. He dedicates this book to the future generations of Detroiters.

◆ 1 ◆
Old Hopes,
New Dreams

A native of Columbia, South Carolina, William Nathaniel "Sunnie" Wilson was born and raised in a city that possesses a unique history among the urban centers of the South. In 1786 Columbia became the state capital by an act of the state legislature which, in an effort to compromise between low- and upcountry planters and merchants, moved the government seat from Charleston to Columbia.

On December 17, 1860, a delegation of South Carolinians met in Columbia's Baptist church to draft the ordinance of secession to leave a union in which they claimed to share "no common bond of interest." Due to an outbreak of smallpox, however, the delegation reconvened in Charleston, where the ordinance was adopted by a unanimous vote of 160 to 0. The first state to leave the Union in 1860, South Carolina precipitated disunion and a civil war in which Southerners fought to uphold states' rights and the peculiar institution of slavery.

When General William Tecumseh Sherman crossed the Congaree River into Columbia on February 17, 1865, his troops met a number of sympathetic whites and free blacks, who served dipperfuls of liquor confiscated from private stores abandoned by city residents. Smoldering cotton bales left in Columbia's streets during the rebel evacuation, along with the drunken carousing of Union troops, started fires that raged across the city. By morning, three-fourths of

15

Columbia was a "mass of blackened chimneys" and "crumbling walls."

For black South Carolinians emancipation and the defeat of the Confederacy represented the beginning of a new era. Though Reconstruction was short-lived in its promise of civil and political equality for blacks, it did, from 1865 until the early 1890s when the racist rule of Governor Ben Tillman began, offer freedoms previously unknown to most black South Carolinians. Upon gaining the right to vote during Reconstruction, blacks in South Carolina established some of the greatest political influence among the former states of the Confederacy. After a biracial delegation drafted a new state constitution in 1868, ten blacks served in the state senate and forty-six were elected to the state house of representatives. In addition to electing two African American lieutenant governors, South Carolinians sent eight black representatives to Congress. These achievements marked the only time in American history that an all-black delegation was elected to the United States House of Representatives.[1]

Under the leadership of Republican governors like Robert K. Scott and Franklin Moses, social change accompanied the emergence of new political freedom. Until Governor Ben "Pitchfork" Tillman's administration and the adoption of a white supremacist state constitution in 1895, black South Carolinians often shared public accommodations with whites. Although most African Americans seeking to test their newfound freedom encountered resistance by whites, Columbia's black population lived in a social atmosphere far more receptive to peaceful relations between the races than in other regions of the Deep South. When room was available, blacks were admitted to Columbia's theaters, concert halls, and other public accommodations. As late as 1885, blacks were served at most bars, soda fountains, and ice-cream parlors.

---

1. Black Reconstruction representatives included Joseph H. Rainey, 1870–1879; Robert C. Delarge, 1871–1873; Robert B. Elliot, 1871–1873; Richard H. Cain, 1873–1875; Alonzo J. Ransier, 1873–1875; and Robert Smalls, 1868–1874. A Civil War hero, Smalls served in the South Carolina state senate and won a U.S. congressional seat in 1876.

The most deeply rooted, far-reaching changes during this period occurred in the areas of religion and education. Reflecting the trend of the larger black community after slavery, black South Carolinians severed their ties with white churches and formed their own congregations. From these independent religious foundations emerged Allen University. Founded in 1870 by the African Methodist Episcopal Church, Allen became the first all-black institution of higher learning established in South Carolina. In addition to theological studies, Allen offered a law department that employed Daniel Augustus Straker, a Barbadian-born graduate of Howard Law School, who became one of the most prominent black lawyers in the state.

Although most of the 780,000 blacks living in South Carolina during the late 1800s remained impoverished and illiterate, Columbia boasted a number of wealthy and educated African American families by 1900. Similar to southern cities like New Orleans and Charleston, Columbia contained a distinct black upper class. As South Carolina's center for African American commerce, Columbia possessed about twenty-five black-owned businesses, such as drugstores, groceries, clothing stores, and barbershops.

Small-business owners and the families of Columbia's religious leaders comprised a population of individuals who left an indelible impression upon young William Wilson. Growing up among the rows of colonial and Victorian houses, shade trees, neatly kept avenues, and in the streets of Columbia's black-bottom sections, Wilson gained firsthand knowledge of the realities and opportunities afforded a young black man during the decade following the First World War—knowledge Wilson utilized in his effort to establish himself in the cities of the industrial North.

I was born on October 7, 1908, in Columbia, South Carolina. We lived in a two-story colonial house located in the middle of Washington, Assembly, Hampton, and Main Streets. My mother, Rebecca, was an attractive woman. She worked as a maid. I don't remember anything about my father.[2] He worked as a Pullman porter; at least that's what my mother told me.

---

2. *City Directory of Columbia, South Carolina, 1927* (Columbia: The State Co. Printer and Pub., 1927), 688. The directory lists Wilson's

My older sister, Irene, had pretty light skin. She was a creole, the tallest person in our family. Since she was six years older than me, Irene would defend me at school. If someone bothered me, she would go after him.

A while later my mother took us to live in the house of my grandparents, the Butlers. We lived downstairs. Grandma Butler was named Priscilla, but we called her 'Silla. She was part American Indian and had long black hair that flowed all the way down her back. My grandfather, Dr. Butler, had jet black skin that made him look like an ancient king. He was a mean man.

Everybody was afraid of the doctor, both the blacks and the whites. He didn't say much to anyone. His eyes stared at me with such intensity that I could barely look into his face. I listened to him and asked few questions. Dr. Butler was into root medicine and was known locally for his herbal remedies. He would send my sister and me into the woods to pick things. "Bring me this root," he'd say. I remember one plant, the Boss Apple. He'd boil it, get the oil out, and put quinine in it. Soon we got to know every tree and root.

Our family always had plenty of food on the table. Every home had a vegetable garden and some had patches that surrounded the entire house. Sometimes my aunt or grandmother would send me out into the yard to bring them a chicken and when I was old enough, they ordered me to break its neck. My sister would prepare it. At hog-killing time, a family would butcher a hog and put the meat in the smokehouse. They usually gave some of the meat to the neighbors. When someone else killed a hog, they would reciprocate. No one went hungry.

Gradually, life with my mother became very hard for me emotionally. Some white show people hired her as maid and took her on the road with them. She was in and out after that. I mostly obeyed my grandmother and my mother's two sisters, Maggie and Emma, who also lived in Columbia. Emma lived where you could raise cows and hogs. Emma was the aggressive one. I liked her, but she worked me too hard. My favorite aunt was my

---

mother, Rebecca, as a cook. William Wilson is listed as employed at the Jerome Hotel at 2116 Hampton Street.

18

mother's younger sister, Maggie. Because of my home life, I chose Maggie to be my new mother. Soon the affection I felt for Maggie became stronger than what I felt for my real mother.

In school I played with both black and white children. Most children didn't go to school, but I liked school. I had white teachers who taught black children and black teachers who taught white children. Unlike students in northern cities like New York and Chicago, we were taught black history from sixth grade until high school. Our history textbook was written by the eminent African American historian Carter G. Woodson. Years later, when I began to tell northern black folks about the death of Crispus Attucks during the Boston Massacre in 1770, they didn't know who I was talking about. After that, I didn't talk much about black history because I didn't want to seem uppity or above other folks who had never been taught their history.

In South Carolina racism was never as bad as Mississippi and other places in the Deep South. Now and again there were some racist individuals and hateful policemen, but for the most part there were good people in South Carolina, including aristocratic wealthy people in big mansions who were part of the southern rebel heritage.

Down there many people were well read. The girls were taught to play violin, piano, and sing in the choir. Most were church-going people. I was reared in both Baptist and Methodist churches. Grandma 'Silla took me every Sunday. Back then you'd go to church in the morning and come back late at night. My family and the older members of the community instilled in me the code of the Southern gentleman—one respects his elders; honors his friends; and one tips his hat to both men and women.

Because of the peaceful race relations in Columbia, it wasn't until I was about sixteen that I realized that I was a Negro. Age sixteen was the breaking point between the races, when you were told to call your white male friends "Master" and the young women "Miss." We didn't think much of it at that time because it had been based upon hundreds of years of tradition.

As a young boy I had red, curly hair. Many people were nasty to me. They called me bad names and I became very mean. There was one boy, Willie White. He didn't like me. Willie called me half-white and everything. He was very black and his name was White so it gave him a complex. Every time we met, we got into a fight. This went on for years until one day I was in a grocery store and heard him call, "Come outside, you half-white bastard." Standing out front of the store I said, "Willie, somebody is going to get hurt. Why?" So we got together and didn't fight any more.

Around this time another thing that caused animosity toward me was that I worked for the lawyers on Washington Street, or what was then informally known as the Lawyer Range. After school I cleaned the offices and tended to the horses of the lawyers. As a court boy I sat near the judge's bench, filling the water glasses of the solicitors. Whenever they needed documents from their offices, I would run and get them. Watching the trials in the courtroom, I learned a lot. Defense lawyers often entered the courtroom holding a Bible. During the proceedings, without opening a page, they would quote at length from scripture. I'd never seen such drama.

Before I entered high school, I worked for the Cooper brothers, John Hughes and Paul. These two white men helped me a great deal. John Hughes, known by many of the white folks as Uncle John, was the older and taller of the two. He had an office on the Lawyer Range, at 1217 Washington Street. John Hughes and his brother graduated from the University of South Carolina Law School in Columbia. After practicing law for a short time with his brother, Paul later founded the Columbia law firm of Cooper & Winter. The Coopers had a feud going back over one hundred years with the Gradys, another lawyer family. Sometimes this feud spilled over into the courtroom and they'd take it out on me and others who worked for them. It could get very demanding working for the Coopers.

There was a lot of prejudice in Columbia, but John Hughes and Paul Cooper liked me. Although I did not know it at the time, when some white Southerners of position recognized certain young blacks possessing intelligence and an industrious attitude, they would help them out. Nobody could bother me, whether they were black, white, blue, or red, because of the Coopers.

Since I didn't have a father, I took the Coopers to be my family. Though the Coopers treated me like family, I was still an employee. John Hughes had a nice home on Taylor Street. When I drove for him, I ate in the kitchen along with their black cook and domestic, a young girl whose quarters were above the riding stable. The only time I ate at the Cooper brothers' table was when I drove them to picnics. Though we didn't dine with the Coopers at their home, we did eat the same finely prepared meals.

Three generations of Coopers lived at their Taylor home. Lawyer Cooper owned an automobile and a horse-drawn, open carriage and I was responsible for driving both, depending on the occasion. Lawyer Cooper's mother still preferred to ride in the carriage and I drove her around Columbia's dirt streets. I pastured the family's horse in a nearby field. The Coopers didn't have a riding saddle, so I rode the horse bareback. On the way to the field, I often met a boy, one of my white friends, who had a horse. We raced the horses up and down the street. One day, when we were coming back from grazing the horse, Lawyer Cooper stood waiting outside the house. He said, "William, I know you've been racing my horse and I want you to stop." He was very upset. I apologized and no more was said between us about the matter.

On Saturday nights Lawyer Cooper gave me the job of standing on the corner of Washington and Assembly Streets in a section of town that stretched all the way down to the Congaree River. This was the black folks' neighborhood—a very mean section where they had whiskey, vice, and gambling. My job was to stand on the corner and if the police raided one of these houses, or if the feds locked somebody up, I'd take their names and call Lawyer Cooper. The next morning he'd go get them out of jail. Sometimes these fellas would give me fifty cents or a dollar for helping them. Lawyer Cooper would take care of me, too, so I became known as Cooper Boy.

When I was about fourteen, I got a summer job working for my Uncle Buster at the Floor Hotel in Greensboro, North Carolina. A sporty fella, Uncle Buster dressed sharp. I liked him and I believe he took a liking to me. I took a train to Greensboro. Just after I began my new job, I was walking home along Macon

21

Street one evening when I passed under a large, steel-truss bridge where the trains passed. When I got to the middle of the entrance under the bridge, a big, burly fella suddenly appeared out of the darkness.

"Stop right there where you are!" he commanded.

"Who are you talking to?" I asked.

"I'm talking to you, you son of a bitch. Don't talk back to me. I'm gonna kill you."

"I . . . ," I stuttered while trying to explain.

"Shut up! I'm gonna give you one more chance. If I catch you going to see Mabel, I'm gonna kill you."

And he kicked me in the seat of my pants. I took off running for about five or six blocks. When I got to Macon Street, I made the corner running as fast as I could. I felt my heart beating wildly as I fell upon the porch. Hearing me arrive, Uncle Buster came outside. He was a big fella. "Let's go get him," he said. "No," I replied, fearful of getting into further trouble. When I went back to work, I discovered there was another waiter there who looked just like me. To my surprise, I found out he was the guy who was seeing Mabel.

One day Uncle Buster told me that he was being transferred to the Floor Hotel in New York. He said I could go to New York if I asked my mother. She agreed and told me to take care of myself. Uncle Buster gave me some money. "Always keep your money in your pockets until you return home," he told me. Then he sent me to New York to live with Miss Baker, my chaperone and landlady.

After I arrived in New York, I got off the train and started looking for Miss Baker's address, 318 Fifty-ninth Street. After taking the subway, I called a cab. When the cab finally pulled up to Miss Baker's, she exclaimed, "What are you doing in a cab? I told your uncle what you should do. Didn't he tell you?" "No," I answered naively. "Well c'mon," she said, leading me to the little room in which I'd be staying. Addressing me in a motherly tone, she warned, "Never go to Harlem. They're bad up there. They may not kidnap you, but they'll beat the hell out of you if you don't have any money."

I didn't know it then, but Fifty-ninth Street was one of the bad streets in New York. It was near San Juan Hill, one of the most crowded areas in the country.[3] That section from Sixtieth to Sixty-fifth was where the gangsters lived.

Since I needed to find a job, I walked up and down San Juan Hill, looking up at the buildings. People could see that I was a stranger. After a while, I got a job at a restaurant around the corner. One day seven white people came in the restaurant. "Can you serve us, son?" one of the gentlemen asked.

"Yes sir," I answered.

"What's your name?"

"William Wilson, but people call me Sunnie. What is your name?" I politely inquired.

"Elmore J. Gould," he responded.

After finishing his meal, Mr. Gould asked if I liked working at the restaurant. I told him I had been working there too long and that I was trying to earn some money to go back to school.

"Where you from?" he asked.

"From Columbia, South Carolina," I said, still unaware of the intention of his questions.

Reaching in his pocket, he took out a card and told me to take it to the Lotus Club. "Don't forget to tell them I sent you," he reminded me.

On a weekday afternoon I went to the address on the card and knocked on the door. A big, West Indian–looking fella approached me. "We don't have any work 'round here. We're not hiring."

"But you haven't heard what I have to say yet," I told him.

"What you got to say, boy?" he said, looking down at me.

"Mr. Gould told me to give you this card."

"Where you know him from?" he demanded.

I told him that I waited on him at the restaurant where I worked. He then instructed me to come back Monday morning.

Monday morning they ushered me in to meet Mr. Lloyd

---

3. Because of the persistent racial conflicts in the district, San Juan Hill, an area stretching from Sixteenth to Sixty-fourth Streets, took its name from the legendary battle site of the Spanish-American War.

Coffer, the head bellman. After being hired as a bellboy, I was measured for a full-dress jacket, hat, and tie. This was quite an experience, because the Lotus Club was a millionaire's club. To be a member you couldn't just earn a million; you had to be born with a million. Elmore J. Gould was damn near a billionaire.

All the members owned yachts. Mr. Gould wore a sailor's cap. When he called, you answered, stood straight, and didn't say anything. Mr. Gould took a liking to me and I took a liking to him. One day he noticed me admiring his suit. He asked, "Do you like this suit?" I said, "I just love it." Then he gave me three or four suits and an overcoat. I had a fur collar put on it. Later, when I attended college, that coat made me the sharpest fella on campus.

Working at the club, I became friends with Lloyd Coffer III, the nephew of the head bellman. He was a heavily built, aristocratic-looking, very well-educated boy who carried a violin under his arm. Lloyd played brilliantly. He came from fine black money. I admired him so much that he became my idol. Noticing my enthusiasm for the violin, Lloyd urged me to buy one and go to school with him. I saved my money and took lessons from Dr. Pendelton on 135th Street. Despite my many hours of practice, I could never learn to play very well; in fact, that instrument damn near whipped me.

About this time I had a pretty, West Indian girlfriend, Vesta, who invited me to her graduation party, a high-society affair held at her home. At the party I was surrounded by her relatives and friends, people of high education and fine manners, who were making speeches in her honor. Feeling intimidated, I soon realized they were going to call on me to speak. I got very nervous. Trying not to be noticed, I stepped out the back door. I looked for a way to leave, but realized there wasn't any access to the street. Finally, I got out the front door and took the subway downtown.

I stayed away from her for a couple of weeks. One day we went to the big rock on 138th Street—the hill in Harlem where they had ice cream parlors and soda stands. Standing beside me, she said, "Sunnie, I want you to do something for me." Suddenly, a nervous jolt went through me. I thought she wanted me to marry her. "What do you want me to do?" I responded. She said, "I want you to go back to school." "But I'm gonna be a musician," I explained, somewhat surprised at her request. "No," she insisted. "I want you to go back to school." All the way home on the subway, she kept repeating her request. Soon afterward, I told my uncle I wanted to go back home so I could finish school.

Due to the extent of my stay in New York, I fell behind the other students at school. I received private tutoring from an older black woman of culture and refinement, Laura Goodman. Down South, women of education and social distinction would, if asked, assist young people in their studies. In fact, I found many black women to be more educated than their male counterparts. With Miss Goodman's help, I was able to catch up with my classmates.

After I graduated from Booker T. Washington High School, I majored in art and drama at Allen University in Columbia. Named after the founder of the A.M.E. Church, Richard Allen, the university was located on the block bounded by Taylor, Hampton, Pine, and Harden Streets. Its red-brick and white-pillared administration buildings faced Harden.

At Allen I was in a variety of plays. Sometimes the teachers would write and direct their own plays. Although I gave up the violin, I was still determined to become a performer. My favorite subject was history. I also enjoyed philosophy, especially great philosophers such as Plato, Aristotle, and Cicero. I liked public speaking and was a decent speaker. The preachers would give us a topic and we would have to expound upon it extemporaneously.

During my years at Allen, I became a member of an informal social club called The Pals, which included my friends Joel Jackson, John McCracklin, T. J. Miles, and Beverly Roundtree. Since we all loved tennis, we got together and built a court in a vacant lot; after a time, I became a good player on the court. T. J. had a car and so did Beverly's parents. We drove to parties and football games. I played football until I hurt my knee. Our opening games of the season were played at Morehouse College in Atlanta, the same day that Spelman, a women's college, held its open house. The Allen team was pretty good, but we weren't much of a match for Morehouse and its tough, four-man offensive line. After the game, the guys in The Pals, known as the girl killers, would dress in their best and go over to Spelman's social just across the way. Established by the Rockefeller family in the 1880s, Spelman had the prettiest black girls in the world. Spelman's prestigious social presented an array of female beauty and since we all dressed sharp, the girls gathered around to meet us.

At Allen I drove for the chancellor of the university, Bishop William David Chappelle. A graduate of Allen, the bishop later became the university's president and the A.M.E. church's minister. He became a bishop in the church in 1912. A big, powerful man with a commanding voice, Bishop Chappelle looked like an African king. Everybody in the black religious world was afraid of him. The white people respected him, including Governor Coleman Blease, the meanest segregationist in South Carolina.

The governor was a tall, aristocratic man who wore wide-brimmed hats. His ancestors were from Liverpool, England. Before he entered politics, Governor Blease had practiced law at the State Supreme Court in Columbia.

In South Carolina, during the twenties, the white folks didn't allow Negroes to buy Cadillacs. Governor Blease told them to sell the bishop a Cadillac and they did. The bishop got whatever he wanted. Blease liked the bishop and he liked Sunnie Wilson. I knew the governor from my days of running errands on the Lawyer Range. The governor had an office on Washington Street, just a few blocks from the capitol building.

One night while driving home outside Orangeburg, I got into an accident and the police arrested me. I had been in Orangeburg to attend a football game at the state college. The car belonged to Dr. Steven, a fella who let the students at Allen borrow it to go to games and the like. On the way back to Columbia, I was driving Dr. Steven's car down the road at dusk and an oncoming car, which had bright magneto lights, came into my lane and hit me. Both cars were completely wrecked. The police came and asked if I had any money on me. After I explained that I didn't, one of the officers said, "Well, what you gonna do about this, boy? You're a reckless driver." I said, "But sir, how do you know? You weren't here." The officer snapped, "Do you know who you're talking to? I'm the sheriff." "Yes sir," I said in a conciliatory manner.

26

He asked me for $250. I told him again that I didn't have any money on me. He then informed that I was going to jail. The police kept my car and threw me in the jail house. This was late on a Friday. I tried to call Lawyer Cooper and couldn't reach him. I called the university and they told Bishop Chappelle.

After being harassed by the sheriff, I spent the night in a cell that looked like a lion's cage. It had brick walls and thick steel bars. The next day the bishop, on his way down to a football game at the state college at Orangeburg, stopped and put up my bail. I then rode with the bishop to the game in Orangeburg.

The authorities were going to sentence me, though, and told me to appear in court. That week I told Governor Blease about it. "They treated me awful bad, governor," I said. "That old sheriff called me bad names. They put me in jail with all those criminals."

The governor agreed to help me. He called the bishop and arranged to have him drive down to the hearing with us. On the day of my court date, the three of us walked in together. The court was already in session. When he recognized the governor, the judge told everybody to rise.

"Good morning, your honor, and good morning, everyone," the governor shouted as we approached the judge's bench. "I just stopped by to say hello. You got my boy Wilson here; you got his car. He's a nice young man, and I have known him a long time. If it would please your honor, I would be obliged if you would give his car back and dismiss the case." "Yes, governor," responded the judge without question. And he threw the case out of court.

During the night I spent in jail, I heard a lot of excited talk in the hall outside my cell. From the conversations of the law officers, I learned that a group of local whites killed Pink Wiley, a black man who had gotten wealthy buying up cotton during the First World War. He had bought up half the town. They killed him and his white bodyguard in a town not far from Orangeburg when he came down from his home in New York to foreclose on a business.

Although my home state went to war in its defense, I knew little about the effects of slavery and its living legend in the South.

The tragic death of Pink Wiley was proof that some whites still hated and feared black folks.

When I drove for the bishop, I traveled on the back roads to various areas around Columbia. He had charges, small one-story churches located in counties throughout South Carolina. It was my job to drive him out to these congregations. Not long afterward, I drove the bishop's wife to Chicago. That's the first time I ever saw Chicago. I'd heard of it because I ordered my shoes from Sears and Roebuck. My friend Maceo came with us. He was a country driver, meaning he knew all the roads and routes through the mountains. I'm a good driver, but I didn't know all the roads.

Finally we got to Mrs. Chappelle's friend's house on South Parkway. When we got there, I asked the maid for directions downtown. Then I rode the bus downtown to look for a job. I traveled up and down the Loop. I met a nice man on the street who asked me where I was heading. After I explained my situation, he told me that they were hiring on the boats in Detroit. So I paid the $1.50 fare and rode the bus eastward to Detroit. I looked around, but I couldn't find any work. Then I returned to Chicago and drove Mrs. Chappelle back to Columbia. But this would not be the last time I would see Mr. Ford's town.

Not long after my return to Columbia, I was encouraged to travel north to Detroit by my Allen classmate Big Tom. Natives of Columbia, Big Tom's parents moved to Detroit. Big Tom told me about Ford's five-dollar day. He wanted me to join him going north to get a job at the Ford Motor Company and informed me that we could stay with his parents.

Encouraged by Big Tom's invitation, I decided to travel north. At that time, my mother took sick. Many people thought she was going to die and they came from miles around, crowding around her bed. I talked to the doctor and he told me she was going to be sick a long time. When I informed my aunts and the visitors that I was going to Detroit, they told me not to leave my mother. But since I had no means of making much money around Columbia, I thought it would be more advantageous to get a high-paying job at Ford and send the money home to help my mother. At that time I owned a cow named Lilly and three pigs.

I milked my cow and sold the milk and butter I made to customers around Columbia. I sold my pigs to pay the thirty-one-dollar fare and still had about ten dollars to spare. On the day I left, my friends gave me a box of fried chicken for the train ride.

I arrived in Detroit in the summer of 1927. This was the first of many summer visits to finance my college tuition. My trip to Detroit was not the usual destination for a young black student from the southeast—from Georgia, South Carolina, and the like. Most of my friends went north to work in New York City, in east-coast resorts, or as porters and waiters on ships that sailed along the Atlantic coast. I, however, remained drawn to Mr. Ford's five-dollar day.

At the Ford factory they sent me to a company man named Wilson. Despite his pleasant attitude concerning the similarity of our last names, he informed me that the company was not hiring. Since Mr. Ford didn't want me, I took a job at the Grey Iron Foundry as a cut-back man, the person on the crew responsible for shoveling back the blackened sand that fell away from the car-body molds. It was hot as hell and we worked hard. I worked there a short time until I got sick.

Next, I got a job at the Detroit Street Car Company. They stocked piles of long contact irons. We had to pick them up, dump in oil, and put them back. When I wasn't doing that, they had us unload ninety-eight-pound bags of cement. By the end of the day, my body was covered with cement dust. But I didn't mind because this job helped build up my muscles. I wanted to get into physical shape to toughen me up for the boxing ring.

I did some boxing back home. I didn't always fare too well in the ring. In South Carolina, I lost in a knockout round; in Savannah, Georgia, a boy known as Tar Baby hit me everywhere except on the bottom of my shoes. But I liked boxing and I needed the twenty-dollar prize money.

After my streetcar job, I worked for the *Detroit News* painting its downtown office building. I learned to paint down South. The majority of the children down South were taught a trade in school. Down there most of the black middle class were carpenters, plasterers, and builders; I was a painter. The *News* paid me

29

about a dollar a day. I slept on the street in newspapers and in the morning I went across the street to a restaurant with a restroom downstairs.

Several summers later, I returned to Detroit with my friend from Columbia, Blanco Woodson. Since we needed money to return to school in the fall, Blanco and I came to town, hoping to find work at Ford. As my luck would have it, they still weren't hiring at the plant. I then went down to the river to find a job on the boats. There were six excursion boats of the Detroit and Cleveland Navigation Company that docked on the Detroit River where Cobo Hall stands today. The D & C hired black cooks, waiters, and bellhops. Its boats sailed from Detroit to Canada, Buffalo, Cleveland, and around the horn to Chicago. Each boat had big state rooms for the wealthy guests and modest rooms for the poorer people. I sailed on the *City of Detroit III*, the *Eastern States*, and the *Western States*.[4]

These boats employed a lot of students who were working their way through law and medical school, like the Pullman porters. I was hired as a bellboy on one of the D & C boats. The fellas on the boat liked me; they got together and bought me a bellhop uniform. I waited on tables, cleaned silverware, and attended to the needs of the guests, who usually tipped you ten cents.

Because the pay on the boats wasn't much, they allowed the workers to gamble down in the hold. The waiters gambled in one place and the bellmen in another. Since I didn't gamble, I often took the place of the fella who was on the night shift. When he wanted to go and gamble, he would call on me.

While sailing to Cleveland one evening, I saw a couple

---

4. Founded as the Detroit and Cleveland Steamboat Company in 1852, the line was reincorporated as the Detroit Steam and Navigation Company in 1868. The D & C's first wooden ships were replaced in the 1880s by four iron steamers. By 1914 the line added four new ships: *Eastern States, Western States, City of Cleveland,* and *City of Detroit III.* From 1924 to 1937 these vessels ran to Chicago on four-day cruises and stopped in each direction at Mackinac Island. In 1926, 438 blacks were employed on the D & C boats, constituting 39 percent of the company's total workforce working on the line.

standing on the deck. After the man's wife retired to their cabin, he stood near the rail and then jumped overboard. The lake's cold, churning water looked dark as death. It dragged that man under without leaving a trace.

Not long afterward on another run to Cleveland, the captain called me up to his office. "Young man, you are a good worker," he said. "You are polite and handle everything in a professional manner, but this is no place for you."

Surprised by his announcement, I told him that I needed the money to go back to school. Nevertheless, the captain was determined to get me off the boat. "Listen, young man," he said in a polite, yet authoritative tone, "you don't gamble, you don't drink. I believe this is a bad environment for you." So he fired me.

To get back to Columbia, Blanco and I bought an old, broken-down Ford touring car for fifty dollars. We fixed it up, put tires on it, and painted it. Driving south through the Cumberland Gap in Kentucky, we encountered a violent rain storm. The downpour was so heavy that we had to pull over to a place and buy canvas panels to enclose the open sides of the car. When night came, the rain continued. We stopped the car in the mountains and slept in the old Ford.

When Blanco and I arose the next morning, we found the storm had broken. We drove on down the mountain until we came to a small roadside cafe. We drove up and the owner came out to meet us.

"Where you boys been?" asked the man.

"Up in those mountains. We had to sleep up there last night," I said.

"I bet you're hungry. Step around back, and I'll get you boys somethin' to eat," said the man.

Blanco and I sat on the stoop and the man brought us out two plates of chicken and rice. Staring down at his plate, Blanco said, "There's a fly in my food."

"What you sayin', boy?" barked the man. "Ma, come on out here. This boy here says there's somethin' wrong with his food."

The woman came to the door and asked, "What's wrong out here?"

"There's a fly in my food," repeated Blanco.

31

I could see by the look on these two people's faces that we were quickly wearing out our welcome. I then attempted to ease the situation by saying, "I have to apologize for my friend. His eyesight isn't so good."

Without any further protest from my friend, we ate the food and quickly departed.

When I went back to Allen that fall, I often worked for the *Palmetto Gleanor,* Columbia's black newspaper. On one occasion, the editor sent me to cover the Teachers' Association convention in Asheville, North Carolina—a large, segregated conference that divided the teachers in two separate halls.

Returning from the conference, I got the idea to hold a weekend dance for the black teachers' association in Columbia. I told The Pals about it and they decided to help me organize a special dance for students and faculty. After securing a large hall that would live up to the approval of the professors and administrators, I borrowed twenty dollars from a friend and hired the best band in town. We sent out invitations to different schools all over the state.

On the night of the affair, we decided to serve punch, so my friends sent me to get the mixer. They told me to buy cherry flavor to put in the lemonade punch. Walking into the drugstore on Main Street, I approached the counter and addressed the tall, white pharmacist, "Doctor, we're making some lemonade punch, and I don't know the exact mix I need. I think it's red."

"You want to make lemonade, and you don't know the color?" barked the pharmacist, looking down at me with a hateful stare.

"No," I replied, "that's what I'm asking you for."

"That's just what I mean about you dumb niggers!"

"I don't understand you," I said, stunned by his reaction. Suddenly an electric charge of anger rose up inside me. "You owe me an apology. I'm a paying customer," I said, looking up into his glaring white face.

"Get the hell out of here!" shouted the pharmacist as he picked up a heavy iron weight from the counter, the kind they used on the scales for weighing things. Thinking the pharmacist was going to hit me with the weight, I quickly grabbed a tall, glass straw holder off one of the tables and threw it at him. It missed him and crashed into the shelves of bottles and jars, creating an explosive sound of shattering glass. I rushed out the side door and instead of heading toward the black neighborhood, I ran down the alley onto Main Street. I could run pretty fast, but when I looked behind me, I saw the pharmacist and a small crowd of white people running after me down Main Street. Turning the corner into my neighborhood, I ran straight into a policeman. "Little Willie, what's wrong with you?" asked the officer.

Just then the crowd arrived, led by the pharmacist who still held the weight in his hand. "See that man?" I said, pointing at the pharmacist. "He tried to assault me." The pharmacist yelled back "He broke the glass in my store. Lock him up, officer!" Since I worked for Lawyer Cooper, I knew the legal terms to present my explanation clearly and intelligently. I told the officer about my party and asked if I could be released.

"Wilson, you're all right," he explained, "but I could never take your word over a white man's." Angered by the officer's statement, I told him to take me to jail. I was in jail only about an hour when my friends came from the hall and put up the twenty-five-dollar bond money.

Back at the hall, the party was about to begin. We had corn-liquor moonshine and we poured some of it in the punch. Outside, I saw a friend of mine, a white policeman, on the corner. I asked if he would watch the door of the hall during the dance. He agreed and I paid him to keep an eye on the crowd entering the hall. We charged a one-dollar admission. Soon pretty black women, students, and teachers began to arrive. Some of the professors attending the convention were interested in the pretty girl students, so they gladly paid the dollar admission. The place was packed.

That Friday night we took in about $490; on Saturday we earned over $300. After closing down the hall early Sunday morning, I went back home to my Aunt Maggie's house. When I greeted my aunt, I was carrying a small valise full of money. I opened it and told her to take what she wanted. She refused.

"You know I raised you better than that. Take that money back," she said sternly, acting as if I had stolen it from the bank.

I could understand her reaction, because most folks down there had never seen that much money in their lives.

"No, you don't understand. I made this money from the dance."

"Oh, God bless you. You have always been a smart boy," she said in a sudden turn of emotion.

She would only accept twelve dollars, but I gave her ten or twelve more.

Monday morning I went to downtown Columbia to put some money in the bank. On the way to the bank, I passed by the courthouse on Washington Street. As I walked by, I noticed that the police were auctioning off cars that had been confiscated from the local bootleggers. Among the automobiles I spotted a big, beautiful Cadillac, a convertible touring car with a spare tire on the back. They were bidding on it, and I immediately responded.

"Ten dollars," shouted the sheriff, opening the bid.

"Twenty," I shouted back.

Someone said thirty, so I said forty.

"You really want this car?" the sheriff asked.

"Oh yes, sir," I replied.

"What you gonna do with it?" he queried.

I told the sheriff that I was a college student and that I needed the car to drive our sports teams to football and baseball games. He then told me that if I wanted it, he would set the bid at fifty dollars.

"Fifty dollars!" shouted the sheriff.

"Fifty-seven dollars!" I shouted back.

Looking across the crowd, the sheriff called out: "Going once, going twice . . . sold for fifty-seven dollars!"

The next day, when I attended chapel service at Allen, the president announced to the crowd that there was a student on campus who, despite owing half his tuition, was driving a Cadillac. "I just drive a little old car and this person owns two cars, a Ford and a Cadillac," he told the crowd. "If he doesn't pay up today, we will have to dismiss him from the school." So I immediately went down and paid my tuition. Nothing more was said.

I got the job of taking the athletes to different schools. Using my Ford and my Cadillac, I charged a fee for each person

I drove to these events. By the time I graduated from Allen, I had saved up enough money to enroll in law school at the University of Detroit. Upon leaving for school in Detroit, I gave Blanco the old Ford that was parked in my backyard. This time I was going to drive to Detroit in style.

◆ 2 ◆
Stage Lights and Nightlife

After Henry Ford's announcement of a five-dollar day in 1914, thousands of blacks headed north, constituting what historians have termed the Great Migration. Claiming only 3,431 blacks in 1894, Detroit witnessed the arrival of 25,000 to 30,000 blacks from 1916 to 1917. These migrant workers, much like the Jewish immigrants of previous decades, took refuge in Detroit's congested east-side ghetto, a thirty-block area bounded by Leland on the north, Macomb on the south, Hastings on the east, and Brush on the west.

In the late twenties Wilson joined the 204,000 blacks who left South Carolina to seek new opportunities in the industrial North. By 1930, 300,000 blacks had emigrated from the South, abandoning their homes and untilled fields. Among the nearly 9,000 blacks who took up residence in Detroit in 1930, Wilson began to establish himself at a time when the city experienced the full impact of an economic depression.

In 1931 Ford's decision to shut down production lines produced a citywide crisis. Thousands of unemployed workers lined up outside the gates of auto plants. One hundred ninety-two thousand received welfare; others walked the streets or took shelter in vacant lots.

As the country fell deeper into the Depression, Detroit's east-side community turned inward from its segregated boundaries to *create both legitimate and illegal economic ventures. Alongside black-owned funeral homes, insurance agencies, and grocery stores, numerous gambling houses and after-hours clubs flourished, attracting black and white patrons. On Hastings, St. Antoine, and Adams Streets, nightclubs featured blues piano men and jazz ensembles.*

Drawn to this colorful nightlife scene, Wilson soon became a member of Detroit's growing entertainment world. His professional manner and ability to deal with the public allowed him to establish connections with some of the city's most important business and community leaders. Befriending politicians, entertainers, and businessmen, Wilson became a prominent member of Detroit's black community.

On my way north to Detroit, I took five passengers in my Cadillac. To help finance my trip, I charged each passenger twenty dollars. They were all young black men looking for work at Ford. Since my Cadillac only got twelve miles a gallon, I needed their money if I was going to make it north of Cincinnati. At that time, white car dealers in the South didn't sell Cadillacs to blacks. I soon learned that they didn't sell them to blacks in Detroit either. When people questioned me about how I acquired my Cadillac, I pointed to my out-of-state license plate and told them that I was a rich farmer's son from South Carolina.

After I enrolled at the University of Detroit to study law, I got a job chauffeuring for Mr. Barber, a white corporate lawyer. I drove Lawyer Barber to his office at the General Motors Building and to vacation spots for the wealthy.

At that time, wealthy whites would take the train to resorts and have their chauffeurs drive their automobiles there. When the Barbers traveled by train to Washington, D.C., and other places, I drove their Cadillac to their vacation spots. While they stayed in the white hotel, Lawyer Barber paid my expenses to stay in a nearby black hotel. If he wanted to golf, I loaded up his golf clubs and drove him to the course.

One time I drove the Barbers to White Sulphur Springs, West Virginia. Famous for its curative mineral springs, the exclusive private resort town near the Virginia border had a luxury hotel, tennis courts, and golf course located on sixty-five hundred acres. It attracted elite folk from throughout North America and Europe—corporate executives and members of royalty. I drove them south through Ohio to the resort at White Sulphur Springs.

The resort hired hundreds of service people and black chauffeurs who wore uniforms ornamented with piping and braids, resembling those of Confederate officers. Along with the rest of the black chauffeurs, I resided at White Sulphur Springs in a long, barracks-style hall. The maids and service women had their own living quarters. The chauffeurs and service people all ate together. After I got to know one of the waiters, he would bring me some of the nice leftovers from the hotel's kitchen. During the day I drove for the Barbers and in my time off, I enjoyed the beautiful mountain scenery that surrounded the resort. It was a pleasant experience.

Since Lawyer Barber paid me quite well, I never let him know I had a Cadillac. In between driving for the Barbers, I studied my lessons on the lawn of the library located across the alley from their home on Massachusetts Street in Highland Park.

As I attended law school and drove for Lawyer Barber, the majority of the boys who rode with me from South Carolina got jobs at Ford. One of these young men worked at Ford in the foundry. Working near the coke ovens, he received severe burns and died. They were going to hold his funeral at St. Stephen's Church on the west side of town.

I went to the church early in the evening. When I got to the doors of the church, a man told me that I had another hour to wait before the funeral started. I asked him where I could get a soda and a piece of pie. He told me to drive around the corner to Bill's Shop. When I walked into the front of the shop, there were two men standing together—the owner, a big Polish fella named Bill, and a piano player named Brown. I walked on past them to the counter in back and ordered a hot dog and a piece of apple pie.

Just after I placed my order, the two men began to argue.

"Give me my change for my cigarettes!" demanded the piano man.

"I gave you your change," exclaimed Bill.

"Oh no you didn't!" retorted Brown.

Pulling out a knife, Brown warned, "If you don't give me my change, I'm going to cut your goddamn nose off!"

While they were arguing, I stood in back by the soda fountain and lunch counter. Because the side exit was blocked, the waitress and I couldn't go anywhere. The black folks who had been in front of the store all scattered to the street. Brown continued to point the knife at Bill, demanding his change. Frightened by the knife, the waitress asked me not to leave. She was a real nice girl. Although I wanted to leave, there wasn't any way I was going to get past those two men.

From behind the counter Bill picked up his pistol. Brown continued to come at Bill. Bill yelled, "Get on out of here!" But Brown kept coming at him. A shot rang out—Bill hit Brown straight in the head. Brown fell to the floor without a sound.

I had seen men shot before. While hunting with a friend in South Carolina, my buddy's rifle went off and shot him in the neck. I remember how he moaned from the wound. But this man didn't utter a sound. He lay stone dead on the floor.

Bill told me to get into the phone booth and call the police. I got inside the phone booth. Still shaken, I began to dial without knowing the phone number. Just as I dialed the operator, the police came storming into the store.

"Come out of there!" commanded one of the officers. "Put your hands up! What did you do it for?"

"Do what?" I asked.

"Kill that man!" said the policeman.

Then Bill explained to the officers that he had shot Brown. One of the officers told me to sit down at one of the tables. The waitress and I sat, while the police looked around the place. They took us down to Vinewood Station to make statements. On the way down I asked the waitress about the store, if it attracted much business. She told me it did quite well. Then I told her to let the owner know that I was interested in buying it.

I told Lawyer Barber about the store and that I planned on purchasing it with my school money. He didn't look on my plan with much favor; he wanted me to stay in school. I called the owner. He wanted $550 for everything, the stock and the like. I bought it and named it The Pals Shop after my friends. Located on Scotten and McGraw, the shop was strictly a soda fountain and ice-cream parlor; I sold no liquor. The ice-cream company put in a new fountain. I dipped so much ice cream my hands turned blue.

A fella by the name of Frank used to come in the shop. A giant black man and brilliant street artist, Frank was a gifted storyteller. I enjoyed having Frank as a friend because when he was in my presence, nobody would dare mess with me. He gave me some of his paintings, beautiful pictures of racehorses. Frank's favorite horse was Black Bess. He liked to do a routine about Bess. Beating his hands on the table to imitate Bess's trot, he would become the announcer. "Here comes Black Bess around the corner!" he'd say, as if calling over a loudspeaker. His act was so good he could make your hair stand on end.

One time Frank came in and set two glasses of water side by side. Using them to represent two individuals, Frank had them boast of their strength. One glass was water and the other wine. Each told how destructive they could be if provoked. "I'm water," said Frank, using one of the glasses. "I can quench your thirst and sustain life. Yet, if I'm angry I can spill over the world and destroy all living things." Taking the other glass, he'd say, "I'm wine, created by the gods. I can raise men's spirits and make them dream. But I can also drive men to madness, causing them to destroy one another."

Frank got sick and became confined to a hospital bed. His legs froze up on him. The doctors never found out his ailment. I went to see him in the hospital. His legs were as stiff as stone. He died not long after. It was sad. Frank was an unknown genius whose stories still live in my mind.

During the first year of business, I did very well. I saved about seven thousand dollars. Although I worked hard, eventually my business began to decline. Another competitor on Millford began to take my business away. After a while, I realized I didn't have too much money left. To keep my lights on and pay my bills, I even had to sell my Cadillac. So I thought of selling the store and moving on to other ventures. My landlady threatened to throw me out if I didn't pay my rent. Since I needed money, a man agreed to buy the store.

Things were pretty bad for me. They were going to cut off the gas and lights in my apartment. My landlady kept my paintings as security. I spent Saturday night quite depressed because they were going to evict me Monday morning. That night a girl I knew sent me an envelope with five dollars inside. She gave me a combination and told me to play it on the numbers. I added five dollars more to it and played a number that was paying seven hundred to one. The results of this particular number didn't come out until Monday.

On Monday morning they were ready to throw me out of my place, when a knock came at my door. I thought it was my landlady. Answering the door, I was surprised to see a man standing before me. I was all packed and ready to leave, but he told me to put back my things. "I got your money," he said, "seven thousand dollars." After I paid my landlady, I told her to go ahead and evict me. The man had told her I had hit the numbers, so she was going to get friendly with me. I told her to keep my pictures, that they were a gift to her, and I left.

With money to invest, I came to the east side where all the prominent businesses and big-time nightclubs were located. Though it had nice homes and neighborhoods, the west side was too quiet for me. On the east side I opened a small company, Long Distance Driving, that drove wealthy people's automobiles to different parts of the country. My idea for starting the business came from my driving experience for Lawyer Barber. If people wanted to go to Florida on the Pullman train car, we drove their automobile down for them, so it would be waiting for them when they arrived. At one point, I had five drivers, clean-cut fellas who wore red chauffeur suits and caps.

Since I could not afford an office, I used Mr. Sidney Barthwell's drugstore on Canfield and Brush as my office and pay station.[1] One of several drugstores owned by Mr. Barthwell, it had

1. A graduate of the 1925 class of Cass Tech High School, Sidney Barthwell, owner of a successful chain of drugstores, opened his first place of business in 1933.

homemade ice cream and a nice lunch counter. I did not know Mr. Barthwell personally. He was my senior—a well-respected wealthy man. I knew his brothers. John worked at the store and let me use the telephone for my business messages.

During my ownership of Long Distance Driving, I lived in an apartment on Canfield. To gain the respect of my peers, I always tried to carry myself with some element of style. My attire included flashy suits, pinstriped and English in style, a derby hat, and, though it was often empty, a leather briefcase. I topped off my look with a small cigar.

At this time, I emerged as just one of a number of black businessmen who sought to establish themselves in the city. But I must admit that when I first came to Detroit, I thought the city would be filled with black businessmen. Initially, I was quite disappointed because I believed these black Northerners had more know-how than my Southern friends in Columbia.

By the time I settled in Detroit, I was pleased to see black businessmen coming together to build a strong community. Various entrepreneurs joined together in black business associations. The Booker T. Washington Trade Association, founded by Reverend William Peck of the A.M.E. Church, and another that held Thursday luncheons were especially effective in the community. Eventually, I became a member of both those organizations. The Thursday meetings assisted black professionals finding work. For example, if a real-estate man needed work, the organization would help him find the proper business connections.

Black businesses sprawled over the east side. Located east of Woodward Avenue and unmarked by official boundaries, Paradise Valley made up the east side's business and entertainment districts, while the residential sections of the lower east side were designated Black Bottom. Back in the 1930s the heart of Paradise Valley centered around Adams and St. Antoine. These streets were filled with action—black-owned clubs, after-hours spots, and restaurants.

When you walked on Adams east from Woodward Avenue toward St. Antoine, you would come to the Lark Grill at 522 Adams, owned by Mr. Robert D. Holloway. A very popular Valley bar and restaurant, the Lark was on the elegant side. Mr.

Holloway was a quiet man and so was his establishment. It served good food and featured a nice upstairs meeting room.

The next eating place, Cookies, on the corner of Adams and St. Antoine, was a good breakfast spot where the entertainers gathered to have ham and eggs after their shows.

Continuing east on the street you'd reach the Norwood Hotel at 550 Adams, owned by Walter J. Norwood, a distinguished numbers-man. In the basement of the Norwood was the Plantation Club. The Plantation catered to elegantly dressed black folks who dined and drank champagne while watching first-class floor shows.

Crossing St. Antoine, you'd hit the Musician's Club and on the same side of the street was Buffalo's Bar, a two-story brick building owned by James Buffalo. In the early 1930s, under Buffalo's proprietorship, the club became a black-and-tan, after-hours place which opened at ten o'clock in the evening and closed at six in the morning. It featured fine piano players. The place catered mostly to white folks because the black folks couldn't afford his prices.

Mr. Buffalo had big pop eyes. He smoked cigars and wore a big diamond ring. Everybody used to argue over whether the diamond was genuine. After he died, someone got hold of it and discovered it was a fake. But no one cared too much because Mr. Buffalo was a popular man in his time, respected by blacks and the rich white people who flocked to his place.

Down from Buffalo's toward Hastings was Club Three Sixes. Named after its address on 666 East Adams, the club, owned by Andrew "Jap" Sneed and managed by Richard King, became one of the finest black-owned nightclubs in the state of Michigan.

Because Sneed looked Asian, the black folks nicknamed him Jap. He had coal-black hair and always dressed sharp in a collar and tie. Sitting with his friends at corner restaurants, he liked to discuss different topics and argue politics. Jap Sneed and his wife lived in Grosse Pointe before it underwent major development.

Before Jap Sneed owned the Three Sixes, he had been in the music-promoting business with bandleader Stutz Anderson of "Stutz Anderson and his Southbound Shufflers." Stutz came to

Detroit from Tuscumbia, Alabama, in 1919 and eventually formed his big band. In 1934 he joined Jap Sneed in the promoting business. Stutz did the footwork and Jap Sneed was the brains of the team, working with the money and investment. Stutz liked to talk about any subject. He wasn't handsome, just a nice-looking, ordinary fella.

Jap Sneed's Three Sixes had a two-foot-high stage and seating for 750 people. Aside from offering first-rate shows with fifteen-piece bands and ten or so pretty chorus girls, the club had fine food. You could buy an excellent steak dinner for six dollars.

Next door to the Three Sixes, Mr. Watson and Grady Jackson invested $200,000 in the construction of the Paradise Bowl, which had a twenty-lane bowling alley, bar, and dining room.[2]

When you turned the corner from Adams onto St. Antoine, heading south toward the river, you'd hit the Pendennis Club. Like most other large cities in the North, blacks in Detroit and their respective organizations owned and operated a number of private clubs. The owner of the Pendennis Club, Mr. Fonney, catered to middle-class members. He was a well-read, sophisticated gentleman, tall and very fine looking. Most black folks thought he was white. His brother, a dentist, passed for white downtown. Mr. Fonney's real-estate investments in the downtown area made him a millionaire.

At 1926 St. Antoine stood the Biltmore Hotel, which featured a downstairs dining room and nightclub. Upstairs was an after-hours spot run by bandleader and violinist Earl Walton. Mr. Walton never had to hire a band because when the musicians got off their gigs, they would come up to his place and jam all night. Although Mr. Walton was a multi-instrumentalist, the violin remained his favorite instrument.

Before the intersection of Beacon was Long's Drug Store. Everybody knew Mr. Long. He owned the only all-night drugstore in Paradise Valley. Next door to Long's, Pekin's Restaurant became the city's finest black-owned eating place. Its proprietors, the Baileys, employed the whole family. The Pekin attracted all the black performers and celebrities who came through Detroit.

---

2. The Paradise Bowl opened in November 1942.

About four doors down past the Beacon stood an office building containing the office of the Watson Investment and Real Estate Company and housing development company, owned by businessman and numbers-man Everett I. Watson. A soft-spoken, respectful man, Mr. Watson was the first black I knew who owned a housing project. Some called him a numbers-man, but I looked upon him as a builder and developer. By the mid-1930s, this building contained the upper-story office of Joe Louis's manager, John Walter Roxborough. This office is where Roxborough handled his investments, strictly a legitimate business, no gambling.

After Watson's and Roxborough's building, you came to Ferguson's Restaurant. Next door to Ferguson's, Benny Ormsby's B & B Fish Dock served only fried fish. Take-out or sit-down, it had wonderful bass and pickerel sandwiches. You could smell the fish cooking down the street.

A little farther south was Roy Lightfoot's B & C Club. A big, jovial man, weighing three hundred pounds, Roy Lightfoot was a real nice fella who loved to laugh. Although the B & C featured good entertainment, its acts were not as exclusive as those billed at the Three Sixes or Plantation.

The southernmost point of interest, on Antoine, was the Band Box. An upstairs gambling spot situated over a poolroom, the Band Box featured what we called the games of chance, blackjack, poker, and the like. The Band Box was not an after-hours place; it existed as a private recreation spot for musicians to meet.

In a small store on 700 East Alexandrine, my friend Fred Allen owned a commercial laundry business, the Supreme Linen and Laundry Company. His business supplied towels for the barbershops and uniforms and tablecloths for the restaurants. Tall, dark, with a pleasant round face, Fred Allen was a lovable gentleman, a man who involved himself with community work. He was member of the National Association for the Advancement of Colored People (NAACP). He liked to play cards and, according to many people, was a good gambler.

His laundry did a tremendous business. He was on the brink of building a business empire. He owned several trucks, which enabled him and his wife to build a nice house on the northeast side near the neighborhood where John Roxborough built his home on Holbrook. I respected his aggressive outlook. He bravely ventured into an area monopolized by the white union and organized by the gangsters. The union men opposed his competition. Although these gangsters damaged his trucks and threatened his customers, he remained unintimidated and continued to build up his business.

He stood his ground until the gangsters decided to hit him hard. One weekend evening, while one of his washers worked alone in the laundry, someone entered the building. The next day they found the washer's body in one of the tubs. Because of the racist nature of the police department, there was never a full investigation and the murderers were never found. Soon Mr. Allen's competitors forced him to close his business.

From my standpoint, I would have fought back against those bastards and let them know they could not use intimidation to stop the emergence of a black business. Despite the shortcomings of his business, Mr. Allen was a black business pioneer and an admirable gentleman.

Unlike Mr. Allen and many of his associates, my first successful start in business happened in an area not fully controlled by whites. Drawn to the bands and nightclubs of Paradise Valley, I began to book shows in different cabarets around town. Each show brought me about twenty-five dollars a night. I hired the musicians and had them rehearse for the shows. I had three bands playing at three different places at once, each with a master of ceremonies, four chorus girls, and a comedian. Back then every show had a comedian to keep you laughing. Together, these acts would play two forty-five-minute shows, each priced at twenty-five dollars, one at nine-thirty and the second around midnight. When they finished their first set, the groups changed clubs, alternating among the three houses. Between performances the entertainers changed clothes and rushed to the next job, which sometimes was miles away. At the end of the night, we met at a restaurant on Vernor Highway and split up the money. I took a percentage based upon my time and investment.

Between clubs and the need for music in after-hours spots, my bands stayed very busy. Through booking acts I was able to purchase another automobile. Sometimes it was hard going, however. I recall one of my bands performed at a blind pig on Alexandrine and Beaubien. They had just finished their show and were waiting outside to get paid. Because I was taking an unusual amount of time rustling up the money, they began to get restless. When the club owner finally paid me, he handed me fifteen dollars and two pints of whiskey. Since it was a twenty-five-dollar job, I said to the owner, "You owe me ten more dollars." "You got your money. You got fifteen dollars and two pints of whiskey," he said gruffly. "What am I going to do with two pints of whiskey?" I asked. "Sell 'em like I do," replied the owner sternly, as if I were naive about the matter.

Meanwhile the band was waiting outside and as every minute passed, I could feel them getting madder and madder. Standing out on the street, I broke the news of the pay situation. Amid the grumbling, I divided up the money. Then, without much protest, we drank up the rest of our pay. It was good, too.

In the late 1920s French-born bandleader Jean Goldkette controlled most of the musical activity in Detroit. When I started booking my small shows, Goldkette still managed the most popular big bands around the city. Goldkette led a hell of a band—Jean Goldkette's Victor Recording Orchestra. His partner, Charlie Horvath, owned the Graystone Ballroom. As a musician, promoter, and co-owner of the National Amusement Corporation, he booked a number of bands, including McKinney's Cotton Pickers, McKinney's Chocolate Dandies, and Jean Goldkette's Orange Blossom Orchestra.

In Detroit the Cotton Pickers played primarily for white audiences in clubs along Woodward Avenue. Like most big bands around the country, such as Fletcher Henderson and Duke Ellington in New York, the Cotton Pickers made big money playing for whites. At that time, a lot of black folks just didn't have the money to spend in expensive ballrooms.

Whenever the Cotton Pickers played a black dance at the Graystone, I was there. The Graystone had two stages and could hold about two thousand dancers. One evening I met the Cotton Pickers' arranger and saxophonist, Don Redman. He was a brilliant and very likable man.

At the Graystone dances you often had to step outside to get a breath of air because the reefer smoke hung in thick clouds. When Louis Armstrong played at the Graystone, everybody in the place smoked reefer, including Louis who stood on stage blowing a number himself. You could get two or three reefers for a nickel. Nobody messed with you; there was no trouble.

Though the Graystone brought in the finest big bands from across the country, it remained the headquarters of the Cotton Pickers. When the Cotton Pickers were in town, they rarely had steady work. So the members were often available for small club dates and the like.[3] I hired many of the band's musicians to play in my bands. Once Jean Goldkette threw a party for Duke Ellington at a place next to the Graystone Ballroom. I had met Duke on my trips to Washington, D.C. Duke invited me to this party, but I told him I didn't have a tuxedo. His first trumpeter Freddie Jenkins, one of my good friends, told me he had two tuxedos and that I could come as his guest. Freddie brought the tuxedo over to my place on Canfield. When I put it on, I felt like a king. I thought Freddie was going to leave it with me, but he came around and asked for it back.

Freddie stayed with Duke until the late 1930s, when he fell ill with tuberculosis. I contacted Duke and urged him to help Freddie out. Though Freddie did not perform with the band, Duke agreed to keep him on the payroll. Years later, Freddie called me from his home in Texas and invited me to move my promotional operations out there. He died not long afterward. Duke loved Freddie and I considered him a great friend.

During the early 1930s, my associations with celebrities and businessmen helped me make a name for myself in the city. In 1933 Morris Wasserman and Sammy Brandt, owners of the

---

3. According to John Chilton, the Cotton Pickers experienced many setbacks by 1931. The loss of its talented arranger, Don Redman, and the failure of the band to renew its recording contract with Victor coincided with the effects of the deepening Depression. At this time the band was forced to work "out-of-the-way venues" that offered reduced pay and attracted scant audiences. John Chilton, *McKinney's Music: A Bio-Discography of McKinney's Cotton Pickers* (London: Bloomsbury Bookshop, 1978), 50.

Harlem Cave, asked me to manage their club. Located on Canfield and Brush, the Harlem Cave got its name because it was
downstairs. It had stucco walls, a good-sized stage, and a seating
capacity of about two hundred people.[4]

Sammy Brandt was born in Russia and arrived in America at
age seven. Mr. Wasserman came from a monied family. His father,
Julius, a Detroit developer and builder, was also born in Russia.
Morris Wasserman owned Wasserman's Loans, a big pawnshop at
3600 Hastings and Rowena.[5] In the late 1940s, he opened the
Flame Show Bar on John R.

Before Prohibition was repealed in 1933, the gangsters ran
the distilleries, manufacturing and selling lightning and corn
whiskey. The club owners ran the speakeasies and blind pigs.
Although there were organizations like the Downriver Gang, the
Hamtramck Gang, and the Irish Gang, the Purple Gang
remained the most powerful operation in the city. Each gang supplied whiskey outlets—clubs and after-hours spots—in different
territories. But the white gangsters didn't dominate everything in
Paradise Valley because there were many powerful black men as
well—mean, tough individuals whom no one dared mess with. In
fact, some of the white gangsters were more afraid of tough black
folks than they were of other white gangsters.

I eventually got to know many of the gangsters because they
often came into the cabarets where I worked. They were big
spenders and tippers. In all my years in the city, I never had any
trouble with the gangsters. They called me Mr. Wilson and
treated me with respect. The Italian don of Detroit was my friend.
Later we used to run into each other on the train to New York
City on our way to watch the fights. He always bet against Joe

---

4. Rollo Vest, *Detroit Tribune*, August 18, 1934, p. 5. The article
reveals Wilson's popularity at the club. Vest writes, "Word comes from
the Harlem Cave that Sunny Wilson is packing them in every night via
his genial personality, wholesome foods, good beer, and great floor
shows."

5. In later years Rowena was named Mack. Morris Wasserman's
Loans is listed in the 1931–1932 *Polk's Detroit City Directory*, vol. 60
(Detroit: R. L. Polk, 1931).

Louis. We were never close friends, but we did have nice, casual conversations. I never asked him about business. I kept my distance. He respected me and I respected him. When the don died years later, I was the only black man invited to his funeral.

Working at the Harlem Cave, I met the boss of the Purple Gang and his lieutenant. Although the Purple Gang was a mean bunch, I got along fine with these two gentlemen. Since Sammy Brandt had married the lieutenant's sister, he often came to the Harlem Cave. One evening while I was working at the Harlem Cave, the lieutenant got into an argument with Kate Francis, a black singer who was the featured act that evening. The lieutenant was a fist fighter. Angered, he turned and slapped Kate in the face. She let out a scream that drew the attention of the whole club. A black-and-tan, the Harlem Cave had a mixed crowd and the black fellas in the place looked as if they were going to tear him apart.

Feeling the crowd grow uneasy, I called over the special police guard who worked for me and told him to hold the crowd while I ushered the lieutenant out into the lounge. After I got the lieutenant into the lounge, I escorted him out the back door into the alley. As the manager, it was my job to keep peace and I did it. Later, Sammy Brandt and his sister both thanked me. I'm sure that if I hadn't acted right away, several people would have lost their lives, including the lieutenant.

Like the nightclubs in Paradise Valley, most of the after-hours spots were black-and-tans—places that catered to black and white customers. There was only one place, a bar in Hamtramck named the Bowery, on Joseph Campau, that wouldn't serve Negroes. Down in the black neighborhoods the majority of the customers in the clubs were white. The after-hours spots had a piano player or a band. The club owners provided food and sold whiskey in tea cups. Some after-hours spots were located upstairs; others were down in basements or crowded rooms. Many of them were beautiful places.

I did one show at a club off Woodward Avenue that had tables with gold-tinted ashtrays and red tablecloths. In my show at this time, I had eight chorus girls and my star entertainer, Sunshine Sammy. The son of a New Orleans chef, Sunshine Sammy

51

was born Ernest Fredric Morrison on December 20, 1912. While his father went to work in Beverly Hills for oil magnate E. L. Doheny, he attracted the attention of the father of child star Baby Marie Osborn, who took him to a Hollywood movie set—an event that let to his appearing in several pictures. Eventually, he became one of Hal Roach's original Little Rascals. As an adult, he entered the vaudeville circuit and became a first-rate dancer and singer. Though he had been on the big screen, Sunshine Sammy remained a down-to-earth, well-liked man.

During this time, as I managed the Harlem Cave and booked my bands, Wasserman and Brandt also selected me to become the Harlem Cave's master of ceremonies. I introduced acts, told jokes, and kicked off the band. They had a five-piece house band led by a handsome trumpeter named Bill Johnson, formerly of McKinney's Cotton Pickers. Often, members of the Cotton Pickers would sit in with the band. In Bill Johnson's group were drummer Freddie Bryant and pianist Sam Price. I hired Price at the Harlem Cave. Originally from Texas, he had worked in Kansas City during the twenties. One day he walked into the club and asked for a job. I liked the way he played and hired him. With Sam Price on piano and Freddie Bryant on drums, Bill Johnson had an outstanding group. I was surrounded by fine talent.

As manager and emcee, I hired acts, mingled with the patrons, and performed on stage. I brought in Sunshine Sammy and we put on quite a show. On stage I used a silver-and-gold baton to lead the bands. It had glass stones that looked like real diamonds. I dressed very sharp and very loud. Sometimes I changed outfits two or three times during a show. While I was backstage, Sunshine Sammy would entertain the crowd. He could do the splits and all sorts of fancy dance steps. He stayed with me until he got into some trouble with the law and had to go back to California.

Back in those days everybody wanted to be a Bojangles Robinson. I first danced in stage plays down South. The average kid down South knew how to dance and many took it very seriously. At the Harlem Cave I honed my skills by watching acts and taking pointers from the champs like Sunshine Sammy and Kid

Williams of Kid Williams and his Harlem Steppers. Sunshine Sammy and I made our entrance dressed in tails. When we danced we put on regular dress coats. Though the band accompanied a dancer, it was the dancer who set the tempo. The drummer followed the dancer. He carefully watched for the dancer's stomp that signaled his break and a display of improvised steps. The drummer also watched for the dancer's spin. When a dancer completed his full turn, the drummer hit a loud accent on the snare drum. On my soft-shoe number, "Me and My Shadow," the drummer used brushes and the muted horns played behind me.

Working on the Harlem Cave stage not only allowed me to dance; it brought me experience as a bandleader. I often started my act slow. If I came on stage and didn't get the proper applause, I would turn around and lead my band, waiting for the music to shake up the crowd. The longer the band played, the stronger the message got. I'd wait for the opportune moment and then I would turn around and play a song the crowd could all sing along with, such as "Let Me Call You Sweetheart." A performer can't beg for applause if he expects to grab the audience. I had to come to them. I had to give them part of myself. My philosophy about entertaining is simple: if you show me a shouting preacher, I'll show you a shouting congregation. I was a shouter.

While at the Harlem Cave around 1934, I met Ella Lee, an unknown talent, who could really dance and sing. I don't know how she got to Detroit or where she was born, but I was determined to make her famous. She was a tall, attractive young woman with a beautiful shape and smooth, jet-black skin. I told her I wanted to make her a star. She agreed to work with me. I took her downtown and bought her three stage dresses—one black, one white, and one red. I helped her rehearse and gain confidence in herself.

The night of the performance at the Harlem Cave, Ella Lee became very nervous. I had everything set for the show. We were all well rehearsed. As emcee I stood in front of the crowd and announced, "Ladies and gentlemen, I want to introduce one of the finest stars in the country, just from New York City, Ella 'Black Beauty' Lee. She is so pretty, folks, I named her Black Beauty." The band started and I announced her entrance, but the stage remained empty. I tried once more, but she did not appear. I told the band to keep playing while I went backstage.

Back in the dressing room I found her crying. She was very upset with me. "Don't you call me black, goddamn you!" she yelled. "I'm no Black Ella." Surprised by her reaction, I explained that it was a stage name, like Black Patti. "You didn't mean it?" she asked. Realizing my sincerity, she decided to perform. A few minutes later she came out in a white dress and excited everybody in the place. I couldn't bring on anyone else. Years later, she retired to have children and opened a beauty shop. Her shop had a sign out front that read "Ella Black Beauty Lee's."

At the Harlem Cave I met a great number of talented and interesting people. One of the people who made my acquaintance was a police lieutenant who lived in Millsboro, Tennessee. A tough but likable fella, the lieutenant had lost his arm to some bootleggers down South. I liked his company so I showed him around town. People often warned me that the lieutenant was bad, but I responded by telling them that I was bad, too. This lieutenant was different from the white Southerners I had met. I felt his sincerity, that he genuinely liked black folks. Just before he left town, he invited me to visit him in Millsboro.

Not long afterward, I got word that my Aunt Maggie was sick. My friend Doc Williams, a West Indian, decided to go with me to Columbia. While driving through Tennessee on our way south, we stopped off to visit the lieutenant in Millsboro. When we got to town, he and his sergeant came to greet us. The lieutenant and I hugged and he took me to meet his family and the city officials. Later we went across the street to the bar in the hotel. Above the noise of the customers, the lieutenant shouted, "Give these gentlemen anything they want!" A woman who ran a little boarding house near the hotel asked me, "Where did you meet the lieutenant? Don't you know that he is one of the meanest men around?" I answered, "That may be true, but he's all right by me."

Later that evening, just before we left Millsboro, the lieutenant told me to avoid the town of Corbin on my way south. "They're bad in Corbin. They don't like colored people," he said. I thanked him for his hospitality and assured him that I had no reason to visit Corbin. I was tired, so I asked Doc to drive. Worn out from the champagne and the carrying on at the bar, I fell asleep.

"Wake up! Wake up!" cried Doc.

"What's wrong?" I asked, half startled.

"Goddamn it!" yelled Doc.

"What the hell you all excited about?" I demanded.

"We just passed the sign! We're in Corbin!" shouted Doc in response.

Since the car was almost out of gas, I told Doc to pull over to the filling station along the road. We parked the car and a white fella walked up to the window. Trying to be as polite as possible, I said, "My car is dry and I'm dry. My lieutenant friend up in Millsboro told me that if I stopped here, you would take care of me." "You know the lieutenant?" inquired the man with a note of surprise. I said, "Yes, of course I know the lieutenant."

Because my driver was dark-skinned, this fella thought I was white. To keep up this deception, I yelled to Doc, "Hey, boy, put some air in the tires and check the oil." My West Indian friend didn't like this treatment at all; he began to get awfully mad at me. I asked the man where I could get a drink and he directed me to a place across the street. Walking through the door, I saw six or seven white men sitting at the bar. I looked around and announced, "My name is Sunnie Wilson from Detroit, Michigan! Let's have a little drink. Give everybody a drink on me!"

These fellas turned out to be quite friendly. When they asked me about my line of work, I told them that I was a real-estate broker. On my way out, one of the fellas said, "Why don't you stick around? We need you down here." I grabbed a pint to go and told everybody to come and visit me in Detroit. Everything turned out fine.

With my success at the Harlem Cave, I began to put together a number of bands. Each featured a singer, comedian, chorus girls, and a soubrette, the lead dancer in charge of the chorus line. I have always maintained that chorus girls bring class to a cabaret. When you see beauty performing in excellent taste, it takes your mind off everything.

Once I rehearsed my shows, I sold them to nightspots for

twenty to twenty-five dollars a night. I had the best musicians in town. When McKinney's Cotton Pickers were not booked, I hired members of the band to play my shows, musicians like trumpeter Bill Johnson, pianist Todd Rhodes, saxophonist Tubby, and drummer Sammy Simpson. Because I hired an emcee for each band, I could appear at different clubs, giving me a chance to emcee shows at various after-hours spots.

Because of the success of my shows around town, a lot of these clubs asked me to take over booking entertainment. I booked musical revues in the Harlem Cave and Mac Ivey's Cozy Corner. But unlike the other clubs, I controlled the payroll at Mac Ivey's. Mr. Ivey gave me the control of the safe and told me to handle the money and the payment of employees. He ran a bar downstairs and a gambling joint upstairs.

After arriving in town from his native Jacksonville, Florida, Mr. Ivey worked in a brass foundry and saved enough money to open a restaurant on Hastings and Alfred in 1919. In 1933 he opened his most successful club, the Cozy Corner. Standing about six feet tall, Mac Ivey was a giant black man, with broad shoulders and massive forearms. He smoked El Producto cigars and carried a .44 revolver under his jacket. Always surrounded by his bouncers, Mac Ivey projected an imposing image. Everybody was afraid of Mac Ivey.

Mac Ivey invited me to run his place not only for my ability to organize musical talent, but because the club needed a major reorganization. I went to work for Mac Ivey on a percentage. If the club didn't make any money, I didn't get paid. Since his employees weren't bringing in any money, I had to make drastic changes. I called all the help to a meeting in the back room.

"My name is Mr. Wilson. Not Sunnie, but Mr. Wilson. How long you been working here?" I asked one of the employees.

"A couple years," he answered.

"And you?" I inquired of another.

"Two years," he responded.

After addressing all the employees, I said, "Good, now you're all fired. I know your record. I've been watching you." All of them looked at me in utter surprise. I eventually hired them all back.

I fired employees when I took over a place; not simply because I was the boss, but to establish a good sense of responsibility among the help. If the staff wasn't making money for the club before I came in, I knew that unless I asserted authority, it would never make money under my management. I told the employees, "Mr. Ivey is the owner of this place, but I am your boss. You will answer to me. If there is anyone here who does not care to work for me, he can leave now. If not, I will hire you back. But remember, I am hiring you, not Mr. Ivey. Now if you plan to stay, sign up on the list that is on the table. For all of you who are going to stay, you will receive a two-dollar raise. But we all have got to go and make some money because my bankroll is not that big." Before long we put Mac Ivey's back in the black.

One of my most successful ventures at this time was an engagement I booked at the Fox Theater. I hired a big band, Sunshine Sammy, a chorus line, a comedian, and two singers, one of whom was George Dewey Washington. He had a great baritone voice that really broke up an audience. For his stage act Dewey Washington covered his body with oil and dressed like a slave in ragged clothes and a battered hat. When he sang "Ole Man River" or "Laugh Clown Laugh," a lament about the lonesome life behind the entertainer's mask, his deep voice brought tears to your eyes.

After the success of this show, I became a star around town overnight. My newfound fame helped get me a two-month job at the Club Balfour at 160 Sproat Street, off Woodward near the old Roxy Theater. Since I had helped Sunshine Sammy get out of jail, he came with me. I bought him several sharp stage outfits. I hired a twelve-piece band and seven chorus girls.

The Balfour was a gorgeous club run by gangsters. I didn't know them personally and I didn't want to know them. There was no need for me to jeopardize their operations. You had to be careful about those things. I didn't want to make enemies with anybody. But they thought so much of me that they offered me the use of the Balfour for a Christmas Eve party. I charged a dollar admission and packed the place.

As I gained a reputation as a manager and producer, club owners began to approach me about running their establishments. On several occasions, numbers-man Benjamin Franklin "Slim" Jones, owner of the Chocolate Bar at 632 Livingstone between Hastings and Beaubien, discussed the trouble he was having running his club. Around 1935 Slim Jones bought the Chocolate Bar from two white gentlemen from Hamtramck. A year later, he came to see me. While I was in the barbershop one afternoon, he walked in and began telling me how his place wasn't making any money. He said, "Mr. Wilson, you've always told me how I could improve business at my place. How would you like to make a go of it?" After I accepted his offer as manager, he handed me the keys to the club and a few hundred dollars. Then he looked at me and said, "I know the first thing you're going to do." "What's that?" I asked. "You're going to fire everybody," he said with an element of humor. "Go ahead and fire everybody," he added, "but don't fire Mrs. Walker, the cashier, because she's my girlfriend."

The first thing I did after dealing with the waitstaff and bartenders was to build a new entrance to the club. The Chocolate Bar, like the Harlem Cave, was located downstairs. To get to the club you entered on the main floor and walked down an entrance halfway across the building. A street-level doorway made the club more accessible to customers as they passed by. I started a cocktail hour and Blue Monday parties. I turned the club's business around.

I told the show producers to bring in some new talent, acts from Cleveland, New York, and other cities. We brought in Detroit bandleader and alto-saxophonist Cecil Lee and instructed him to rehearse every day. Mr. Lee was a fine musician, a quiet unassuming man, who had played with McKinney's Cotton Pickers and Lanky Bowman's band. I brought in Herb Jeffries—the Detroit-born singer who later went to Hollywood and became the Bronze Buckaroo, the singing black cowboy. Herb was a slim, good-looking young man with a fine voice. Oddly enough, he didn't seem to care about becoming a great singer; I sensed he wanted to do something else with his talent. He wanted to become a movie-star cowboy. Years later, Herb made it to the big screen and became a star.

Another notable who sang and played for me at the Chocolate Bar was Dave Wilborn of the McKinney's Cotton Pickers. He entertained my customers on his banjo. Everybody liked to hear him sing his theme song, "I Want a Little Girl."

During my stay at the Chocolate Bar, my friend Leonard Reed worked the Plantation, located on Adams, in the basement of the Norwood Hotel. Though he wasn't much of a performer or pianist, Leonard was the finest producer I ever met. He was extremely intelligent and a comical man. Leonard was very light-complected. That worked against him, because he was too light to pass for colored and too dark to pass for white. He and Joe Louis were very close friends. He taught Joe how to play golf and dance. He and Joe even worked up a tap dance act together. Sometimes they would get up on stage at the Rhumboogie in Chicago to show off their routine. Leonard and Joe often came over to the Chocolate Bar and I went to visit them at the Plantation.

While managing the Chocolate Bar, I courted Leonard's soubrette. When we went on dates, I asked her to tell me about the shows they were working on over at the Plantation. I don't think this young lady knew what I was up to and she gladly told me the details of Leonard's shows. Back then the chorus lines' choreography changed the shows every couple of weeks. I stole Leonard's shows and opened my acts with the same performances. Since each club held matinee shows, the producers attended each other's performances. When Leonard and I sat together at the Chocolate Bar, he would say, "Goddamn it! That looks just like my show." Leonard knew I was stealing from him, but he had no hard feelings because we were good friends. Although I was a better emcee and could outdance Leonard, he remained a far superior producer. It was all show business. When Sally Rand, the famous fan dancer, came to the Bonstell Playhouse on Woodward, I stole from her show, too.

Allen University in my hometown of Columbia, South Carolina, where I earned a bachelor's degree in art and drama. (Photo by Gretta Abu-Isa.)

The *City of Detroit III*, one of several lake boats of the Detroit and Cleveland line on which I worked a summer to earn my college tuition. (Courtesy Burton Historical Collection.)

Many black-owned businesses thrived on the east side during the 1930s and early 1940s. Andrew "Jap" Sneed's Three Sixes on Adams was one of the finest nightclubs in the state of Michigan.

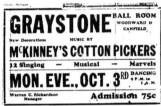

At Monday Night dances at the Graystone Ballroom, black folks gathered to hear big bands, from McKinney's Cotton Pickers to acts like Louis Armstrong.

Fred Allen, my longtime friend, owned and operated one of the most successful black-owned laundry businesses in Detroit.

For many years, jovial 300-pound Roy Lightfoot owned the B & C Club on Adams (c. 1937).

Raising a toast to nightclub owner Roy Lightfoot when he defeated me during my re-election campaign for Mayor of Paradise Valley.

After working in several clubs, I became manager of Slim Jones's Chocolate Bar (c. 1936).

Heavyweight champion Joe Louis, my greatest and most humble friend, during his heyday. (Courtesy Burton Historical Collection.)

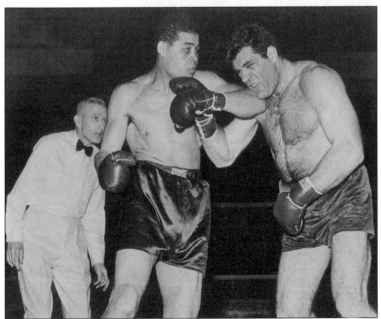

In the ring Joe stalked his opponents. He was a knock-out man. (Courtesy Burton Historical Collection.)

Here I'm with several of our good friends at Joe's training camp at Pompton Lakes, New Jersey. From left to right, Charlie Glenn (seated in the first row), Walter Douglas, and Woogie Harris is behind me. To my left, holding the bottle, is St. Louis Kelly, Joe Ziggy Johnson (in back), and Ed Small.

At the Chicken Shack, Joe and I celebrate his winning the heavyweight title in 1937.

Outside the Chicken Shack
with my head waitress.

In 1937 Joe formed the second Brown Bombers softball team. Pictured in
the first row (from left to right): Beefin' Bill, Blue Lewis, Charlie Brown,
L. C. Lockett, Buddy Stevens, Alex Childs (in back), Julius Redmond,
Hubert Paine, Albert Tate, Charles Hutchins, Ben Raiford (in back), Shorty
Ross, Hollie Larkins, Earl Witherspoon, and Country Davis.

The Brown Bomber's Chicken Shack was a gathering spot for a number of celebrities, like Duke Ellington's vocalist, Ivie Anderson (fourth from the right). To my right is Detroit newspaper journalist and writer Ulysses S. Boykin.

A happy gathering at the Chicken Shack (c. late 1930s).

With my friends Marva Louis and nightclub owner Jap Sneed (c. 1945).

In 1939 Joe purchased Springhill Farm, a 447-acre horse farm in Utica (Shelby Township), Michigan. I wanted Joe to turn the farm into a resort, "Joe Louisville," but Joe's manager John Roxborough opposed the idea. Joe was a fine rider and could really make a horse gait. (Courtesy Burton Historical Collection.)

• 3 •
Mayor of the Valley

My passion for show business has always coexisted with a love for politics. When I began to establish myself in the east-side community in the early 1930s, the majority of black folks in Detroit supported the Republican Party. In 1930 the black community elected Charles Anthony Roxborough, who became the first black Michigan senator to be elected by an all-black constituency. Roxborough graduated from Detroit College of Law and, after becoming a lawyer, entered into a long and successful career in Republican politics.

Beginning with President Roosevelt's second term in 1936, black Detroiters, like most black folks around the country, threw their support behind the Democrats. Though I never remained a staunch party advocate, I began my early years as a Democrat. I worked with a group of Democrats who invited me to help them promote their candidates. The group included Emmitt Cunningham, Frank Owens, and Charles Diggs Sr., who became Michigan's first black Democratic state senator in 1936. Before I participated in the group's efforts, Charles Diggs and Attorney Bledsoe teamed up with Attorney Joseph Craigen to form the Michigan Federated Democratic Club, the first all-black Democratic organization in the country. These men were my elders and I was pleased they invited me to assist them in promoting their campaigns.

Unlike most of the other associates in the group, Harold Bledsoe and I struck up a close friendship. I enjoyed listening to his philosophy of life and business. He was born in Texas, educated at Howard University and earned his law degree from the University of Michigan. After being admitted to the bar in 1925, Bledsoe became a member of the firm of Lewis and Rowlette. He assisted in the defense of noted Detroit black physician Dr. Ossian Sweet in the famous Sweet case of 1926 that upheld the right that "a man's home is his castle."[1] Bledsoe's colleagues called him the black Darrow. In defending a client he created such a tension that you swore a silent breeze was blowing through the courtroom. His oratory and presentation were unmatched in the city. Though Bledsoe's dream of becoming a judge was never realized, his vision was not in vain. His daughter and son both became judges.

Back in the 1930s, though Detroit had several prominent attorneys like Charles Mahoney and Cecil Rowlette, the state and county governments had no black judges. During those days many black folks of notoriety were entrepreneurs or numbers operators. Most didn't have time or the opportunity to go into

---

1. Dr. Ossian Sweet was a successful Detroit gynecologist who had trained at Howard and Wilberforce Universities and completed postgraduate courses at the Universities of Paris and Vienna. In 1926 Dr. Sweet purchased a home in a white neighborhood on Garland Avenue When the Sweet family moved into their house on September 8, a mob gathered outside. The next evening a larger crowd assembled and began throwing stones at the Sweet home. In the residence Sweet, two brothers, a student from Wilberforce, and six other men armed themselves in defense against the crowd. A shot from the defenders killed one bystander and wounded another.

The National Association for the Advancement of Colored People (NAACP) took up Dr. Sweet's defense and brought in famed defense lawyer Clarence Darrow as counsel for the defense. Judge Frank Murphy presided over the case. Darrow's defense was based on the sociological tactics of racial injustice and self-defense. He declared in the courtroom: "If eleven whites had shot and killed a black while protecting their home and their lives against a mob of blacks . . . they would have been given a medal instead." Following a brief deliberation, the jury acquitted Dr. Sweet and the other defendants.

law or politics. I joined our group of Democrats in running Charles R. A. Smith for a judgeship in the Recorders Court. During the early 1930s, Charles R. A. Smith served as the city's first black assistant prosecuting attorney. A native Detroiter, Mr. Smith was educated in a private Catholic school. Later, he graduated from Northwestern Law School and opened a local practice in the 1930s. This was the first time a black man ran for judgeship in the city of Detroit.

When we met Mr. Smith, he impressed us as a forthright and polished gentleman with a reputable and moral background. A humble and reserved individual, he was married and had two daughters, Sarah and Viola. To run for Recorders Court he had to, in accordance with the Hatch Act, resign his government office as assistant prosecutor. Initially, our campaign was greeted by cheers and enthusiasm. Our Democratic committee appointed me head of fund raising and publicity. I looked upon this opportunity as a privilege and I worked day and night to promote the campaign. The *Detroit Times* gave us a great deal of vital publicity. Though R. A. Smith won the primary, many black folks began to argue that the time was not right to run a black man for a judgeship in the city; many of our early supporters abandoned the campaign. On the day of the election, not enough blacks turned out to vote for Smith. Thus, in effect, they defeated their own candidate. But Smith remained a man we all admired for leaving a well-paying job to support our cause. He will always be remembered as a trailblazer who paved the way for Detroit's black judges.

Though I was involved in mainstream politics, I sought to help the east-side community by running as the unofficial mayor of Paradise Valley. In the early 1930s I was elected one of the first mayors of Paradise Valley.

To promote a sense of community, the black people of Paradise Valley elected an unofficial mayor. Rollo Vest, a newspaperman with the *Detroit Tribune,* came up with the idea as a promotional event to sell newspapers. He ran a contest that promised the winner a date with Duke Ellington's singer Ivie Anderson, and a term as mayor of the Valley. Every two or three years a new mayor was selected through a newspaper poll. The mayors of

Paradise Valley were businessmen: Roy Lightfoot was a nightclub owner, Rubin Patton, a car salesman, Chester Rentie, a booking agent, and Albert "Geechie" Pakeman, an employee of the Goldfarb bail bond agency.

The inauguration ceremonies included an extravagant ball held at the Graystone Ballroom. Duke Ellington's band was hired by the black business community to provide the entertainment for the dance. The Graystone inauguration ceremony required that the new mayor elect participate in a mock marriage proposal to Mrs. Anderson. She was a beautiful, stylish singer who loved music. Although Mr. Vest initially organized this ceremony as a promotional idea for the newspaper, it soon became a regular event.

I was elected mayor in the 1930s. As part of the celebration activities, the loser had to push the new mayor down Hastings Street in a wheelbarrow from Beacon all the way down to Gratiot. This part of the inauguration could become serious, such as when I ran against Roy Lightfoot, the owner of the B & C Club. Roy Lightfoot beat me in the next election and I had to push all three hundred pounds of him up Hastings. To make things even more difficult for me, Roy Lightfoot sat toward the back of that damned wheelbarrow. As I struggled to push him up the street, he just sat there with a big smile on his face.

At that time, the black population of the east side was a closely knit community. Relations among our people were fine. There was very little violence. If someone got robbed, the criminals would leave him a dollar to get home. Hard drugs were almost unknown. Dope and opium remained within small, inconspicuous circles. The majority of the fellas smoked reefers. Prostitutes working the turf in Paradise Valley were required by law to take physical examinations at the Board of Health. The community had organization.

If two young fellas in the neighborhood had a dispute, they met at the playground in front of the Brewster Center. Each took along his second, a back-up person who kept his man from being kicked while he was down. The two put on their gloves and settled the matter—no knives or pistols, just fists. The loser shook the winner's hand and they parted. There was no major violence because the people of the black neighborhoods watched out for each other.

As mayor of the Valley, I met with the politicians to seek ways to improve the conditions of the black community. We worked to educate and register blacks to vote. I visited community centers and handed out goodwill baskets to the poor black folks. I didn't want any special favors as mayor, no special job or money. I became mayor strictly to help out my fellow black folks in Paradise Valley. Many people called me an activist for my public actions, and in many ways I lived up to that image. I saw white landlords put out black families with small children in the ice and snow. I couldn't tolerate such treatment, so I got four or five of my friends together, mostly prizefighters, and told the landlords to put the people back in their apartments.

When the Jewish restaurant and deli owners along Hastings practiced a policy of discrimination, I fought back. I did not have any personal dislike for Jewish people, but I could not tolerate the racist practices of these individuals. These owners served Negroes solely on a take-out basis, meaning you could place your order at the counter but could not sit down with the white customers and eat your meal. In retaliation, I had some fellas get up on the roof of the buildings across the street and throw rocks to break their windows. If a place continued to prohibit the seating of black customers, they would repeat the process.

I don't consider myself a gangster and do not advocate violence, but I believe this tactic was justified. Some of my Jewish friends called and told me these owners wanted to talk to me. I explained to them that Detroit was not South Carolina. I said, "We order in these places and we will eat in these places." I think they were intimidated because they thought we were going to burn their places down. Anyhow, they agreed to our terms.

Though black Detroiters began to gain the right to eat in white restaurants, they were still denied means for attaining loans from white banks. The only way for blacks to enter business was to borrow money from loan sharks or loan companies. These operations usually offered five-year loans at 10 percent interest a year, often adding 6 or 8 percent on top of the yearly interest. Black businessmen could not afford such high interest rates.

For black Detroiters during this time, the most important source of economic and political power rested upon the numbers operations. I was never interested in getting into the numbers. They just never moved me. One of my close friends always advised me to stay out and I did. I was more interested in promoting my bands and running my own business. However, my friends who did go into the numbers became millionaires.

Originated by black folks, the numbers became a very lucrative business in Detroit. The city had several houses that handled policy, a lottery game based upon the numbers obtained by shaking a container of small tubes with the numbers inside. The winning numbers were based upon three digits. Policy houses in Paradise Valley were run solely by black operators. The Purple Gang didn't bother venturing into the numbers. A white mob from Cleveland tried to come and take over, but they were run out of town by my Irish friend, Police Inspector Morgan.

If you wanted to play policy, you had to contact a black numbers-man. They weren't hard to find; they operated all over town. The pick-up numbers-men had their own districts and solicited business in their respective areas. They picked up your number in the morning and later that day, the numbers runners distributed a sheet listing the winning digits. You checked to see if you hit the right combination. If your numbers matched, they brought you the money the same day.

The money made by the numbers benefitted the black community; it might circulate for weeks before it left the black folks' neighborhood. Someone would win a dollar and it would go to the bar; the bar owner might spend it at a restaurant and then that dollar would go to the grocery store and so on. The longer that dollar stayed in the neighborhood, the better the economic situation. This kind of economic turnover can make a city boom.

The numbers games were essential for the progress of black folks in the city of Detroit economically and politically. Blacks used this money to build housing. They founded insurance companies, loan offices, newspapers, and real-estate firms. The numbers bought the Walter Norwood's Norwood Hotel and Slim Jones's Chocolate Bar. Numbers money also helped create scholarships for young people to attend school and served as housing down payments. Black numbers-men like Joe Louis's manager, John Roxborough, and Everett Watson, owner of the Watson Investment and Real Estate Company, were my friends. Since they were my seniors, I never socialized with these gentlemen. I never saw them turn any numbers.

The importance of numbers in the community was revealed in a story told to me by Walter Norwood. He used to take money from his hotel and his numbers operation to the bank. Walking down the street, a Chinese gentleman approached and asked him what he had in the bag. "I've got black folks' dreams," answered Walter Norwood. Not long after, he saw the Chinese man on the street. This time the Chinese man was holding a bag of his own money. He told Walter Norwood, "Chinese people got black dreams too."

Policy existed as a business. Since numbers-men didn't want any trouble, they refused to allow criminals to get involved in their operations. One numbers-man, Policy Geech, was so honest that the black folks of the Valley just loved him. If 3-6-9 came out that day, he immediately paid the winners off. This man acquired the name Geech because in Louisiana and South Carolina, black folks who spoke with an island dialect or accent, be it Jamaican or the creole speech of the Gullah people of South Carolina, were called Geech or Geechie. Policy Geech spoke with an accent and ran policy, so he became Policy Geech. When he went broke, he went back to driving a truck and hauling steel. A tough individual, Policy Geech was one of the only black men they allowed in the teamsters' union. But he didn't need much money to get back into the numbers business because he always obeyed the system of honorable debt: his word was his bond.

In the 1930s a group of white gangsters met with the black numbers-men to discuss the possibility of a merger between them. Often, black numbers runners were drawn away from their community by the monetary rewards offered by the white gangsters. This incentive caused many to go to work for white operators. At this meeting the white gangsters planned a takeover of the black numbers-men. Mr. Everett Watson attended the meeting surrounded by his bodyguards and told them all to "go to hell."

Black Detroiters also gathered in private clubs to play black-jack and poker. These clubs had private charters and you had to be a member to gain admittance. The Pendennis Club on St. Antoine offered gambling upstairs. The Waiters and Bellman's Club on Gratiot, owned by Mr. Watson, featured blackjack and poker. Sometimes an undercover man would come in and that's when the police would raid the club. I was never a member of these clubs, but I often attended them as a guest of other members.

Many of my associates in different cities were in numbers. These individuals were very successful. Their children went to college and many became doctors, lawyers, and so on. Among my friends in the policy business were the Jones Boys of Chicago—Mack, George, and Ed. These brothers made millions in the numbers. All of them were good-looking and very intelligent. As a young man I loved to spend money. The Jones Boys enjoyed watching me spend money and liked to give me cash. I didn't care where they got it as long as I could spend it.

Mack used to call me on the phone and say, "Hey, Sunnie, what are you doing?" "I'm not doing a damn thing," I'd answer. He'd say, "Get a plane and come on over here." He would send the money for the ticket and I would head for Chicago.

One time I was sitting in a place with George when he called for his chauffeur to pull the car around front. I asked George, "What do you want to ride for? The place we're going is just a few blocks." He said, "It's too hot out there. Let's take the car." I told him, "No man, let's walk." Confused by my request, George asked, "Why do you want to walk in this weather?" "Listen," I told him, "you're a millionaire. I want to walk with you so people think I'm rich, too."

In Chicago the Joneses ran policy out of milk depots. They owned hotels and Ben Franklin stores. They were very enterprising individuals, far different than any blacks I had known up to that time. The family owned a chateau in France. Their daughters spoke French and Spanish. The Jones boys acquired the European manner of kissing each other when they greeted and departed. The numbers made them multimillionaires. After their

68

father died, their mother was the backbone of the outfit and Ed was the boss.[2]

I spent so much time in Chicago that many of the local folks thought I lived there. While in town I visited all the South Side clubs, such as the Grand Terrace on South Parkway, where I met pianist Earl Hines, and the breakfast dance held at Mike Delisa's Club Delisa on State Street. I liked Chicago, but for some reason I never had the desire to live there. Detroit was my home.

Like Chicago, the numbers flourished in Detroit. They operated without much interruption until August of 1939, when a white woman, Mrs. Janet McDonald, committed suicide. This woman and her boyfriend, William McBride, were in the race-horse and numbers businesses. Upset over her breakup with McBride, Mrs. McDonald took her daughter to a garage near her home, where she closed the door and asphyxiated herself and her daughter with the automobile exhaust fumes. When they found the bodies, the investigators discovered confidential information exposing the city's numbers operators. Once the authorities started the investigation they couldn't stop it. It became a political event.

To investigate the case, a twelve-man committee petitioned to appoint Judge Homer Ferguson a one-man grand jury, known as "Judge Homer Ferguson's one-man, graft-gambling grand jury." Judge Ferguson and his investigative staff found that members of the police force and city government had accepted ten million dollars a year from policy operators. As a one-man grand jury, Ferguson indicted Mayor Richard Reading and his son and former secretary, Richard W. Reading Jr., along with 132 others,

---

2. According to Mr. Wilson, all the Jones boys led tough lives. Ed Jones went to prison for income-tax evasion, where he found himself at the mercy of white gangsters. This continued after his release, as the gangsters extorted money from Jones's numbers operation and kidnapped his brothers George and Mac, forcing him to pay a ransom. While driving to a cabaret one evening, Mac Jones hit an embankment and died. Not long after, George Jones received an empty coffin at his home, which was a message from white gangsters warning him to cease his numbers operations. He was so frightened that he moved to Mexico.

including Mr. Roxborough and Mr. Watson. Beginning in the fall of 1939, the Ferguson grand jury led a six-month search to find Mr. Watson. In February 1940 the authorities located him in a Chicago suburb, living with his wife Irene Watson and heavy-weight fighter Roscoe Toles. They extradited Mr. Watson and brought him back to Detroit to face the Ferguson grand jury.

Following the indictment of Mr. Watson, the authorities went after Mr. Roxborough. But Mr. Roxborough's indictment and conviction need not have happened. Roxborough knew Lavert "St. Louis" Kelly, a powerful black man and friend of Joe Louis. St. Louis Kelly headed Chicago's Local 444 of the Colored Bartenders and Waiters Union. St. Louis was a little thin man who weighed about 135 pounds. Years before, in St. Louis, he had gotten into a fight with a fella and received a knife slash on the back of his neck. After he killed the man, folks around St. Louis called him Cutneck Kelly. Because of his trouble with the law, Mr. Kelly left St. Louis for Chicago and became head of a service workers' union. He was a powerful figure on the South Side. He put pickets outside Club Delisa, forcing its white owner to hire black waitresses. Whenever one of the Jones boys was kidnapped, he would have his men go get him back. He ruled the South Side until a man named Cat Eyes finally killed him.

Though the public looked upon Mr. Kelly as a mean and dangerous man, Joe and I both viewed him as a gentleman and a friend. He liked to follow Joe around.

Mr. Kelly was a friend of Homer Ferguson's prosecutor, who lived in Niles, Michigan. He and Mr. Kelly used to hunt together. During their association, this prosecutor imparted con-fidential information to Mr. Kelly, including information con-cerning the Ferguson grand jury. Upon discovering the inside track concerning Mr. Roxborough's fate, Mr. Kelly felt that it was his duty to warn him. While I was in New York, Mr. Kelly instructed me to tell Mr. Roxborough that if he didn't get in touch with him by the next day, they authorities were going to send him to the penitentiary. So I walked into the Nemo Club in Harlem to find Mr. Roxborough. I found him and his wife sitting at a table together.

I said, "Mr. Roxborough may I talk to you in private?"

He replied, "No, boy! I'm here with my wife." He referred to all of us around Joe as his boys. A member of a powerful family, he was the boss. Though many others called him Johnny or Roxie, I always addressed him as Mr. Roxborough. As my senior, Mr. Roxborough deserved my respect.

"But this is confidential," I explained.

He sternly inquired, "What is it?"

I suddenly became vexed by Mr. Roxborough's attitude and his inclination to humiliate me in front of his wife. Standing in front of the table, I said, "Mr. Kelly told me to tell you that if you don't get in touch with him by tomorrow at this time, you're going to jail. I'm not talking too loud, am I?"

Then I walked over to the bar and ordered some champagne. Mr. Roxborough got up from the table and walked over to where I was sitting.

He said, "Sunnie, my wife told me I was too raw with you."

"I've always respected you," I said. "I didn't want you to belittle me in front of your wife. Mr. Kelly told me to deliver a message and I did."

Mr. John Walter Roxborough was a high-class gentleman gambler, a powerful numbers-man. He was a man of few words, a serious and well-read man. Born the son of a lawyer in Plaqemine, Louisiana, Mr. Roxborough came to Detroit with his family in 1899. Attending Eastern High School, John and his brother Charles Roxborough played basketball on the Eastern City Championship team of 1905. Mr. Roxborough attended the University of Detroit on an athletic scholarship.

In later years, however, John and Charles did not associate with the same crowd. They viewed each other with resentment, each looking upon the other as an outlaw. As a politician Charles Roxborough carried the greatest weight. His brother smoked his cigars and didn't let anybody intimidate him.

Being from a prestigious family, Mr. Roxborough made his own decisions. He never called St. Louis Kelly and he went to jail. In Detroit Circuit Court on January 7, 1942, Judge Earl G. Pugsley convicted Mayor Reading, Mr. Roxborough, and Mr. Watson. Although sentenced to four to five years in prison, Mayor Reading maintained his innocence. Immediately following Mayor

71

Reading's sentencing, Mr. Roxborough and Watson were given two-and-a-half to five-year terms. Despite Mr. Roxborough's intransigence, I believe he and Mr. Watson were singled out by the investigation in order to set an example.

The city's attempt to break up the numbers hurt the economic condition of the black community. Black Detroiters saw the trial as a direct attack on their community. Though it may have forced many numbers-men temporarily to curb their operations, the Ferguson grand jury never entirely stamped out gambling in the city. After the white members of city hall took gambling away from the black folks, they later legalized it and called it the state lottery. The only difference between the black folks' policy and the state-run lottery is that we had three digits and the current game has six. Today, the state-run lotteries take in a national total of 361 billion dollars a year, but there are no black men running the lottery in Lansing.

Later, policy was replaced by the mutual, a game which drew its winning numbers from the closing figures of the New York Stock Exchange. Controlled by white gangsters in New York, this game ultimately took over the black numbers operations.

Throughout the first half of the 1930s, however, numbers financed black business and made the boxing career of Joe Louis. Without John Roxborough's money, Joe would never have become the world-class fighter we know today. Roxborough's management made possible a great number of opportunities for Joe and his friends, including myself, to participate in events which live in fond memory and the history of our people.

◆ 4 ◆
The Twenty-Dollar Man

When they appeared together in public, the towering Joe Louis and diminutive Sunnie Wilson made a striking combination. A somewhat unique, yet not unlikely pair, Louis and Wilson traveled together throughout the United States and the Caribbean, meeting many of the most famous entertainers and businessmen in the world. Six years Wilson's junior, Louis admired his older friend, a person famous for his congeniality and first-class sense of fashion. Though known by many as Louis's running buddy, Wilson shared more than good times with the heavyweight champion. Unlike millions of fans, Wilson witnessed firsthand the triumphs and tribulations of an international sports legend.

Born on May 13, 1914, in a small, wood-framed house located near the base of Alabama's Buckalew Mountains, Joe Louis Barrow grew up in Chambers County, an area known for its red soil and towering pine trees. In 1926 Louis's stepfather Pat Brooks, in search of industrial employment, brought the family's nine children by train to Detroit and settled them in an eight-room house on Macomb Street. Soon after, Brooks moved the family into a tenement on Catherine Street. During his youth, Louis drove a horse-drawn wagon, delivering ice in Black Bottom with his friend, and later personal secretary, Freddie Guinyard.

With money given to him by his mother to pay for private violin lessons and wages earned cleaning floors at his older sister

73

Emmarell Davis's home, Louis trained at the Brewster Recreation Center. Under the tutelage of Alter Ellis he became a Detroit Golden Gloves champion. Louis's boyhood friend Thurston McKinney was one of many fighters who was managed by Sunnie Wilson. Known around town as a promotional whiz, Wilson was introduced to the young, up-and-coming Louis in the early 1930s, initiating what became a lifelong friendship of mutual admiration.

Joe was one of the finest individuals I ever met, from the beginning to the end. He was always a gentleman and humble, and being humble made him great. He harbored no malice and never exerted his authority in public. He was a great emancipator and he brought more people together than I have ever known, black and white. Out of respect, Joe never called me Sunnie. He always called me Mr. Wilson. Joe was my partner and friend to the end until the Great Master called him.

I met Joe during the early 1930s, when I was promoting the Golden Gloves. As one of Michigan's first black boxing promoters, I helped start Detroit's Golden Gloves. We had a gym in the basement of the Ebenezer A.M.E. Church on First and Willis. The church was a nice establishment that moved to the location in 1936.

I presided over a funeral service there once. A friend of mine and I vowed that if one of us died, the survivor would give the service. This fella died of a gunshot wound to the stomach. Having some preaching experience from down South, I put on a frock coat with tails and gave the service.

Around 1936, our Golden Gloves activities at Ebenezer helped get young men off the street and offered them a healthy competitive environment. It was where many young boys trained. Several black churches like Mt. Olive Baptist sponsored baseball, basketball, and boxing teams.

My first experience as a boxing promoter emerged in a roundabout fashion. At the time I lived in an apartment on Canfield. Every street had a boss, a tough fella who knew how to use his fists. The boss of Hastings Street, Jack Boyd, boasted that he could knock out Archer, the boss of Canfield. Noting that their rivalry brought attention to the residents around Black Bottom,

I realized the potential for making a little money on it. I then contacted Jack Boyd and Archer and told them, "Don't get in trouble fighting on the street. Let me set up the match, and I'll promote it for you." I offered each 25 percent of the take to participate in a bout at the Ebenezer Church gym. I told them I needed 50 percent to cover costs of the advertisements and so forth. They agreed.

Word of the fight got around and the night of the fight, people packed the gym. Unknown to me, somebody informed the police about my not having a license to run the event. At the church gym everything was going according to schedule. The fighters arrived with their gloves and their seconds. Near fight time two policemen came in. One approached me and asked, "Do you know where I can find Sunnie Wilson?" "Sunnie Wilson? I think he went up the stairs over there," I said. "You know he's running this event without a license," informed the officer. "The last I saw him he went that way," I repeated, pointing toward the stairs.

When the policemen walked into the crowd, I hurried out the door carrying the money. I told the fella taking the money at the door to keep the rest of the proceeds and to tell the fighters to meet me at the Harlem Cave, owned by my former employer, Morris Wasserman, who knew all the local police. Later, Jack Boyd and Archer came into the club to collect their money. The winner, Jack Boyd, demanded more money. To avoid an argument, I handed him another ten dollars. I made out quite well on my take and the police never did locate Sunnie Wilson.

After the Boyd-Archer fight, I acquired a boxing license and promoted such local talents as Shug and Buddy Waterman, Leroy Willis, Bubba Shipp, Dave and Albert Clarke, Clinton Bridges and Thurston McKinney. One of the most handsome boxers I have ever known, Thurston moved in the ring just like Ray Robinson. Thurston got Joe Louis interested in boxing. He took Joe down to the gym in Brewster Recreational Center. Thurston's fighting name was Punchy. Joe Louis named his son after him.

Under my management Thurston fought a bout in 1936 that grew out of a rivalry he had going with fighter Milton Shivers. Thurston and Milton didn't like each other. So they scheduled a fight between them at the Arena Gardens, a white-owned place that had a bar and restaurant located at 5797 Woodward Avenue. This bout was one of those fights where the winner takes all, not the prizefighter but those with the winning bets. I put my money on Thurston.

Though Thurston was determined to get Milton, he stayed on the ropes during the second round. Milton tried to catch him. He pounded Thurston with punches from corner to corner. Milton was a bad boy. By about the eighth round, Thurston danced around the ring until Milton cut him with a left and then a right. Milton's blows knocked Thurston out of the ropes. I yelled, "Get up, Punchy!" All my money was on Thurston. So I kept repeating "Please get up, Punchy!" But he just lay there while the referee made the count. The worst part of it is that I forgot to fill the car up on the way over to the fight. So when I drove Punchy back along Woodward Avenue, the car ran out of gas, and we had to walk all the way back to the Chicken Shack. I was so mad I didn't speak to him.

For a while I signed a contract to promote fights at the Arena Gardens. I hired a black referee and an announcer. But before long, the black people I invited to the place began to complain that the management refused to serve them alcohol. Many asked me, "Sunnie, why did you bring us to this racist place?" Since my customers didn't like the place, I stopped promoting fights there. Every time I saw the owner, he tried to apologize. I just curtly told him, "Get out of my damn face!"

In my spare hours I would go down and watch the young boxers spar at the Brewster Recreation Center. Since I was a promoter and was known around town, Joe wanted to meet me. From the very beginning we found that we shared many similar interests: boxing, pretty girls, automobiles, horses, and cowboy pictures. Right from the beginning, I was struck by the sincerity of this young man. He didn't dream of becoming a big celebrity. He was just human, just plain Joe. He loved his family and he strove to make them proud of him.

Joe's managers, John Roxborough and Julian Black from Chicago, were both numbers-men, intelligent individuals who ran a tight ship. Before managing Joe, Mr. Roxborough had been director of the Dunbar Athletic Club's boxing program. Later he trained his boxers at the Brewster Recreation Center.

After Mr. Roxborough moved Joe's base of operations from the Brewster Recreation Center to Chicago's Trafton Gym in 1934, the champ often returned to Detroit by train. The Chicago-Detroit run was known as the Four-Forty-Five because it took only four hours and forty-five minutes between destinations. I usually joined the fellas to meet the Four-Forty-Five at the station. As he got off the train, Joe gave people in the crowd a dollar, and others he knew five or ten dollars. But he always gave me a twenty. They called me the twenty-dollar man. Not long ago Mayor Coleman Young asked me why he only got two dollars and I got twenty. I told my friend, who was just a young man at that time, "'Cause you were just a little fella and I was a big fella."

I frequently visited Joe's New Jersey training camps, first in Lakewood and later in Pompton Lakes. Because of the lack of privacy at Lakewood, Joe's managers moved his camp to a more secluded spot at Pompton Lakes on the grounds of a former private estate. So many of Joe's fans and curious onlookers came around that eventually guards were placed at the estate's entrance. Joe stayed in a two-story, tree-shaded house. I relaxed by playing cards and reading the newspaper. Sometimes Joe and I would sit and have dinner together in the mess hall. At the camp I'd work out to keep up my health. Joe would get up at six in the morning and run six or seven miles before breakfast. Sometimes I'd run with Joe or hit the bags. Out of respect, Joe never let any of the fellas in the camp swear in front of me. He told everyone to call me "Mr. Wilson." Soon they all began calling me "The Reverend."

President Roosevelt often visited Joe at Pompton Lakes. The president was a big fan of Joe's. He rode around the camp on a golf cart followed by a entourage of secret servicemen.[1]

When Joe was scheduled to fight Max Schmeling in 1936, the president and the American public looked to him to score a

---

1. Despite President Roosevelt's affection for the boxing champion, Louis campaigned for the Republican candidates in the 1940 and 1944 presidential elections.

victory against German fascism. Despite the fact that Schmeling never joined the Nazi Party, Hitler promoted him as symbol of the German superman. Schmeling had nothing against Joe personally. Years later the two became friends. On June 19, 1936, in New York City, Schmeling knocked Joe out in the twelfth round. Joe couldn't believe it and neither could anybody else. A man of few words, Joe didn't say much to anyone. He just said, "I'm gonna get him next time." He felt like a little boy who had lost his sheep. The loss didn't surprise me, though. Joe had just gotten married to Marva Trotter—a beautiful young woman from Chicago—and was too busy having a good time. He didn't listen to his trainers, and because he didn't consider Schmeling a real threat, he became over-confident. After the fight, Joe and his trainers had to be protected because many thought the bout had been thrown. While the Germans applauded their hero, the black folks remained angry at their hero's defeat.

Joe lost some pride and prestige, but he never gave in. I believe the first Schmeling fight served as the biggest lesson of his career. After that he trained hard. He looked upon each opponent as a potential champion. I had told him repeatedly, "Whenever you fight, you've got to be prepared." After the fight, he went home to visit his mother and Marva in Detroit. At Lillie's he relaxed and met with friends. While he got himself back together, Joe vowed to redeem himself.

As Joe overcame the effects of the first Schmeling fight, he and Leonard Reed invited me to manage their restaurant, Leonard Reed's Chicken Shack at 424 East Vernor Highway. So I quit my job and went to work for Joe and Leonard. It was Leonard who had the idea to open a chicken shack and Joe agreed to back him. According to Leonard, Joe, through Mr. Roxborough's backing, laid out ten thousand dollars without a written contract. Joe wasn't really interested in the restaurant—all he wanted was a place for his friends to gather. After Leonard hurt his back in a car accident on his way to California, he gave me his share of the business. Subsequently, I bought Mr. Roxborough out and Joe and I renamed the restaurant the Brown Bomber's Chicken Shack.

I became the owner two hours before midnight on New

Year's Eve 1936. That evening, we held a grand-opening celebration. Joe bought us all tuxedos. When we raised our champagne glasses at midnight, I ushered in the new year as the owner of the Brown Bomber's Chicken Shack.

At the Chicken Shack I served the best fried chicken in town. My cook, Fats, could fry up twenty orders in fifteen minutes. During our first year, we had three delivery trucks. We even invested in Brown Bomber's Chicken Shack II, a small take-out place across town.

The Chicken Shack had valet parking and an outside patio. The club had a white piano that all the great pianomen signed, including my good friend Duke Ellington. When Duke came for an appearance in Detroit, I had him and his wife stay at my apartment on Vernor. I would get myself a room so they could have the place to themselves. My home was his home. I had a piano in my den. One night Duke kept getting up from it. He paced the floor for hours, humming in a low voice. Great composers rarely sleep. Their minds, like those of most gifted thinkers, are always working on new ideas. Duke walked and talked music. During one of our conversations, he told me the next great music was going to be made by women. He was a very serious man. I observed Duke Ellington, his manners and poise. Genius, cultural refinement, gentlemanly disposition—these were the qualities of Mr. Duke Ellington. His title was fitting. He was the duke.

A great number of celebrities came to the Chicken Shack. One night the Marx Brothers and I sat together on the patio. When movie stars Robert Preston and Sylvia Sidney played the Michigan Theater, news got out that they were coming to my place after the performance. From the patio I saw people get out of their cars and crowds gathering on the street, so many that the police blocked off Vernor Highway. Robert Preston and Sylvia Sidney arrived by car. Ms. Sidney was a short, beautiful woman. When the cast arrived, we had a hell of a party.

Other notables who came to the Chicken Shack included Louis Armstrong, Jack Dempsey, Walter Winchell, Milton Berle, Dorothy Lamour, and Cab Calloway. I first met Cab in New York at the Cotton Club. He married one of the Cotton Club dancers. Years later, he told me that people had predicted that the marriage wouldn't last a year. But his wife stayed by his side until his death. When he visited Detroit in the 1940s, I took Cab for a cruise on the Detroit River. The Stroh family often loaned me their yacht and its captain to take celebrities on the river. We sailed from the marina on Belle Isle up and down the river. One night while I had a party on the Stroh's yacht, Cab began to sing a slow, pretty ballad. I said, "Damn it boy, I didn't think you knew how to sing." I only knew Cab as a showman, and I didn't consider "Hi dee hi dee ho" singing. But on this particular night, Cab proved his talent to me.

Another time I took Cab over to the Eastwood Gardens Amusement Park. We both decided to go on one of those rides that swing way up in the air. It about scared the hell out of us. When the ride came down, he said to the ride operator, "Goddamn it, let us out of here."

Cab didn't like Milton Berle, and one evening at the Chicken Shack they exchanged harsh words across the room. I thought they were going to get in a fight. Both of them were outgoing and loud individuals. Perhaps they were too much alike. Nothing came of it, though—just words. I saw Milton Berle later and we just laughed it off.

As owner of the Chicken Shack, I got involved in a humorous, alcohol-related incident myself. After closing the bar Easter morning, instead of going straight home, I stayed around drinking rum and colas with my friend Pete Fischer, a tall Detroit deputy-sheriff lieutenant from Texas. Outside on the street we were quite intoxicated. I was wearing a white hat and Pete reached over and snatched it off my head. I jumped up and snatched his hat. Speaking to me in a drunken Texas drawl, he said, "Give me back my hat, or I'll lock you up." I told him to go ahead, and he pulled out his handcuffs and cuffed my wrist to his. Then he began to pull me, causing the metal cuff to cut into my wrist. As he led me around, I started hitting him with my free hand.

Just then a police car approached. "What are you doing there?" inquired the officer of my friend. "Why, I'm taking this man to jail. He's drunk," Pete replied. Discovering our condition, the policeman told Pete, "Take those handcuffs off him."

Pete responded humorously, "What do you know, I left the damn key at home."

Unamused by our drunken behavior, the officer told us both to get in the patrol car. He drove us to the police station. They threatened to fire Pete. I think we both learned a lesson. I never drank rum and colas again. Since that Easter morning, I have remained strictly a champagne man.

Another one of my customers at the Chicken Shack was Bill "Bojangles" Robinson, the famous dancer. Bill Robinson was a tough individual. A friend of mine, a white fella, Mr. Frank Barbaro, owned a popular club in Hamtramck, the Bowery, which brought in a lot of big-time acts. My friend booked Bill Robinson for a show. Robinson invited Mr. Roxborough and his friends to the performance. He asked them to come backstage. When the owner saw Bill Robinson with all these fellas, he said, "I didn't bring you out here to entertain your friends. I brought you here to dance." Bill Robinson told him, "Well, give me my money!" This man gave him the money. I'm glad he gave him the money, because Bill Robinson had a permit to carry a pistol. He always carried a pistol.

Nineteen thirty-seven proved a year of great achievement for Joe Louis. On June 22, he defeated James Braddock in an eight-round knockout to win the heavyweight championship of the world. I was at ringside when Joe knocked out Braddock. The whites cheered for Joe as much as the blacks. Late that summer, Joe traveled with the Brown Bombers softball team on a West Coast tour. Formed in 1936,[2] the team, made up of Joe's school buddies and friends from Black Bottom, emerged out of a neighborhood youth team, the Duffield Midgets, winners of the 1930

---

2. Under the management of pitcher Otis Stanley, the original Brown Bombers team roster read: Leo Perry, pitcher; Simon Larkins, catcher; Joe Louis and Ben Raiford, first; Robert Nelson, second; Hubert "Fats Stuff" Paine, third; Hollie Larkins, shortstop; Gus Adams, short center; Julius Redmond, outfield; Earl Witherspoon, center field; Milton Buyers, right field; and John Carlyle and Walter Johnson in reserve.

city recreational softball title. Based at the Duffield School playground, members of the team befriended Joe when he lived across the street from the school.

Though Joe sponsored the team, he did not play with the Brown Bombers until he won the heavyweight title in 1937. That year, he provided money that made it possible to acquire top players from around the city to purchase handsome brown-on-brown pin-striped uniforms and a tour bus. But Joe's New York promoter Mike Jacobs did not approve of his boxer playing softball. During his first game with the Brown Bombers one of the players from the opposing team stepped on Joe's foot, causing him to fall to the ground. When Jacobs learned about this, he lay down the law. Gus Adams, one of the original Brown Bombers, recalled how Jacobs called and informed the team that if they "let Joe play another game, I'm gonna have you all killed!" After that, Joe's playing was restricted to one-inning appearances.

Between bouts Joe played with the Brown Bombers at Detroit home games at Mack Park and Hamtramck Stadium. The Brown Bombers played in Flint and Pontiac, where they went up against the Pontiac Big Six. Joe appeared with the team at parks and prisons all over the country—in Cleveland, Chicago, Charleston, West Virginia; Uniontown, Pennsylvania; Los Angeles; and ballparks in Canada.

I traveled with Joe when he played on the team, introducing him to the wardens and officials. While visiting Jackson Prison, I accidentally walked into the place carrying Joe's pistol. He had given it to me and I had forgotten about it being in my pocket. I walked in and out of Jackson and they never knew I had a pistol on me.

On one of the trips with the team, Joe and I took the train out of Chicago to a town in Wisconsin. When we got to the station in Wisconsin, the train was late and the game had already started. The sheriff came down to take us to the ballpark. The sheriff was determined to get us to the game and sped past the traffic. I told the sheriff that I had always wanted to sound a police siren. "Where's the siren, officer?" I asked. "Right here," he answered pointing to the switch. I reached over and turned on the siren, letting it scream all the way to the ballpark.

During Joe's 1938 rematch with Schmeling, he knocked out his German opponent in the first round, striking a powerful blow against Hitler's racist ideology. His victory over Schmeling made him an international hero. Like Jesse Owens at the 1936 Berlin Olympics, Joe upset Hitler's quest for racial superiority.

In the months that followed, Joe and I enjoyed many good times together. One day Joe and his wife Marva came to visit me at the Chicken Shack. When they came in, I was with my girl Anna Lee Simpson. We were sitting having dinner when Joe invited me to see his new Mercury convertible, a gift from the Ford Motor Company. Joe was always receiving gifts from various companies. In the middle of dinner he said, "Hey man, let's try the car out." I said, "Okay, let's all go." He then told me that he wanted to take a ride without the girls.

So we left Anna Lee and Marva in the Chicken Shack and jumped into the Mercury. Driving down the highway, I noticed we were traveling a far distance from the Chicken Shack. Sensing Joe was up to something, I asked, "Where we going?" "We are going to Toledo," he said. "They have a big chorus-line show with beautiful girls." Then Joe asked me how much money I had on me. I reached in my pocket and took out seven hundred dollars. Joe had twelve hundred dollars or more. "But what about our girls?" I asked. "They can wait. We are going to Toledo," he responded.

That night we drove to Toledo. From there we went to Cleveland and then drove to a friend's farm eight or nine miles outside the city. In need of money we drove back to Cleveland to borrow some from friends. After buying some new clothes, we resumed our trip. On the way to New York City, we stopped in Buffalo to visit Marshall Miles. Since we never called anyone, Mr. Roxborough and Marva were becoming very worried. Believing us missing, they were ready to contact the FBI. Unknown to us, President Roosevelt had been trying to locate Joe to open the March of Dimes campaign in Washington.

We saw Joe's personal secretary, Freddie Guinyard, in Buffalo one morning. Freddie was actually Joe's advance man, helping to make contacts and set up ticket sales for Joe's fights. As a boy, Freddie worked on the ice wagon making deliveries with Joe.

They were old friends. Freddie provided Joe with companionship on the road. He told Joe jokes and kept him laughing.

When Freddie saw us in Buffalo, he called Mr. Roxborough and told him of our whereabouts. Without a word to anyone, we continued to Albany, New York, where we pulled into town, cold and hungry from driving through the mountains. I asked someone where we could get a drink and a steak dinner. They directed us to a black-owned bar and restaurant. Worn out from the road, Joe decided to wait in the car while I went in to check the place out. I stepped up to the bar and ordered some champagne and a side of brandy. A loud, boisterous fella, the bartender began to tell of his visits to New York and how he had made friends with celebrities like Bojangles Robinson.

I said, "I know Bill Robinson."

"Sure you do," the bartender replied sarcastically. "I bet you know Ethel Waters too," he continued.

"Yeah, I know Ethel and her man, Eddie Mallory the bandleader."[3]

"You don't know any Bill Robinson or Ethel Waters," said the bartender.

"Sure I do and I have Joe Louis outside in the car."

"The hell you do," said the bartender, nearly laughing.

"Well, I need two steak dinners."

"I don't have any steak. You'll have to get a hamburger at the corner."

I was becoming very impatient with this fella. I told him, "I'm sitting here drinking champagne. I don't want a hamburger."

Joe had fallen asleep in the car. I was about to go out and get him when he came walking through the door. When he caught sight of Joe walking into his place, this fella's jaw about dropped to the floor.

"Where's our steak?" asked Joe.

---

3. Chicago-born trumpeter/saxophonist/arranger Eddie Mallory was briefly married to singer Ethel Waters and served as her band director from 1935 to 1939.

I informed Joe, "We're not getting any. This fella says we'll have to grab a hamburger at the corner."

"Okay, let's go get a hamburger," said Joe.

"No fellas, I was just kiddin'. Me and your partner here were just havin' a little fun," desperately explained the bartender.

"No thanks, we're going to the corner," I said, "and I hope next time you'll learn to watch your damn mouth."

Soon afterward, Joe got word of President Roosevelt's invitation. Since Joe had an appointment in New York City, we headed there and after buying new clothes, took an airplane to Washington, D.C. When we arrived at the airport, security men were waiting to greet us.

Joe and I needed to use the restroom. Standing in the lobby, I saw four restrooms—one for the white ladies, one for the colored ladies, one for the white men, and one for the colored men. It outraged me to see these signs of segregation in our nation's capital. At that time, Washington was a very prejudiced town, and in defiance of its segregation laws, I led Joe straight into the white men's restroom. Seeing us enter, the black washroom attendant said, "Hey, you ain't supposed to . . ."

"Shut up, boy," I said. "Get us some towels." And we walked out as if nothing had happened. Being a humble young man, Joe remained silent, although he opposed segregation as much as I did. I was the bad guy who refused to keep his mouth shut.

Washington, D.C., was more segregated than South Carolina. At least in South Carolina blacks had a separate section in the theater or a restaurant. We called the theater's segregated upper balcony "the buzzard roof." In Washington black folks couldn't enter white movie houses or theaters. The only white-owned place where blacks could eat was Union Station.

Joe asked the secret servicemen if they could drive us to see the Lincoln Memorial. We got in the car and to our surprise, the car dropped us off at the Howard Theater, in the heart of the black neighborhood. Angered that we were not provided with first-class accommodations in the white section, we checked into the colored hotel, got dressed, and went to the White House to meet the president.

The president liked Joe and often asked him to appear at public events. On one occasion, he invited Joe to lay a wreath at President Abraham Lincoln's tomb for a Veterans' Day celebration. Joe and I attended the ceremony along with a crowd of old black and white soldiers from the Civil War and the Spanish-American War. Since I had met the president several times before, I was determined to express my opposition to Washington's segregation laws. Joe was the quiet one; I was the aggressive one. Since the president liked Joe, I knew that I could voice my opinion without causing any animosity.

Walking up to shake his hand, I leaned over and whispered: "Mr. President, we could have gotten arrested today for going into the wrong restroom. You've got to do something about this situation." The president turned his head to one side and answered in a soft voice, "Well, I'll see what I can do about that."

We were gone two weeks. My girl didn't want to speak to me for months. Mr. Roxborough didn't want to know me and Freddie Guinyard thought it was my fault. But it was Joe's fault, not mine. He wanted to follow that show clear to Albany.

To get on speaking terms with Marva, Joe bought her a fur coat. Marva was a dignified and beautiful woman. When Joe first met her she had been taking courses at the University of Chicago and at a school of design. Being young and in the spotlight, I don't believe Joe knew what he had with Marva. A woman who loved clothes, Marva dressed wonderfully. When they were seen in public Marva and Joe were a handsome couple. Marva added grace and sophistication to Joe's life. But Joe's passion for lovely chorus girls often led him to neglect the responsibilities of marriage.

Joe's interest in show girls took us on regular trips to Atlantic City. When he wasn't busy fighting or on a tour, Joe traveled with me back and forth between New York, Washington, and Atlantic City. Since the trains ran every couple of hours, we commuted between the three cities. To promote my show name and help cover expenses on the road, I'd often get weekend club dates as an emcee. Whenever I was in Washington, D.C., I stopped in at the Howard Theater and asked the manager for an emcee job.

These gigs helped me to get exposure. Years later, when a newspaper interviewer asked why I didn't make it in show business, I answered, "No one laughed at my jokes."

Joe and I had good times in Atlantic City. It had two large cabarets with big chorus-girl shows: The Paradise in the black section and the largest one, Mr. Williams's place, on Main Street. The Paradise handled nationally known acts. In the late 1940s he booked saxophonist Illinois Jacquet, hired my friend Joe Ziggy as producer, and periodically featured Larry Steele as the emcee. In later years Mr. Williams featured stars like Frank Sinatra, Tony Bennett, and Ray Charles and his Raylettes. Mr. Williams had gambling in the back room. On one of the walls of the club he hung a racehorse tote board. The club was adorned with beautiful draperies. In the evenings, when the club opened to the public, Mr. Williams hid the board by drawing a curtain over it.

When Joe and I went to Atlantic City, we usually headed straight for the chorus-girl shows at Mr. Williams's place, except the time Joe fought Tony "Two Ton" Galento in 1939. Galento broke several of Joe's ribs. That weekend, Joe didn't do anything but stay in his hotel room.

To accommodate Marva during her stay in Atlantic City, Joe eventually bought her a nice house there from Ma Robinson. An upper-class woman from Philadelphia, Ma Robinson always wore diamonds and some called her Diamond Lil. She had a nice house in Philadelphia with a bar in the basement. Her place had the prettiest girls I have ever seen. Marva and Joe liked Miss Robinson. Even after Joe bought the house, he continued to stay at hotels in Atlantic City because he liked to go out and play with the girls.

During one of our trips to Atlantic City, Joe took Marva and I escorted my girl Anna Lee. A few days later, we decided to send the girls home by plane so we could watch the chorus-girl shows together. Anxious to get our girls to the airport, I really pressed on the gas pedal. The car was speeding about twenty miles out of Atlantic City when a police car pulled us over.

"Hello, young man. Do you know you were driving seventy-five miles an hour?" asked the officer, looking down at me in the driver's seat.

"I told him to slow down, officer," said Joe from the back seat.

"Is that Joe Louis you got in there?" inquired the surprised officer.

"Yes sir, I work for him," I responded.

"Well, I guess you don't care who you kill," said the officer. "Where is your chauffeur's license?" queried the officer, losing patience with my cool manner.

"I don't have a chauffeur's license," I responded. "I'm Joe's friend and I'm taking him to the airport."

"Not right now you're not. Turn your car around and follow me," demanded the officer.

Standing before the magistrate, the officer presented me as "the speeder who tried to kill Joe Louis."

"So you're the one who drives for Joe," said the magistrate. "You seem to be a decent young fella. Can you stand to lose fifty dollars?"

"Yes, sir," I politely answered.

Because of his respect for Joe, the magistrate let me off easy. Later, after I paid the fine, I took Joe aside and said, "Now give my fifty dollars back."

In Atlantic City Joe and I took time to enjoy the ocean. We often chartered a fishing boat. Under the instruction of the crew we would cast our lines down into the water. Out on the boat, we'd cook our catch down in the hold.

But the waters of Atlantic City also recall a far more traumatic incident. One time we went to the beach with a group of people. While Joe and his friends were sitting together, I went for a swim. Although I considered myself a good swimmer, I had never been in the ocean. Not knowing the power of the waves, I dove into the water. Every time I tried to come up, a wave pulled me back under the water. Finally, the flow of the waves carried me back towards shore. When I got on dry land, I was so wiped out that I had to crawl back to where Joe and the others were sitting. They were busy having a good time and never noticed my predicament in the water.

While we were all sitting together, I noticed a little girl wandering out towards the waves. I immediately jumped up and ran to her as she walked into the water. The whole beach greeted me as a hero when I brought her back. They all treated me as the greatest thing you've ever seen. But what they didn't know is that I was almost a dead hero.

Joe and I spent a lot of time together in New York City. While we stayed in Harlem, we visited all the nightclub spots—all the places that featured beautiful chorus girls, like Small's Paradise, the Randolph Bar, and the Nemo Club. In New York I sat in and sang a few songs at the Nemo Club and a place across the street where Billy Eckstine led the house band.

Mr. Eckstine was my friend. I first met him when he was selling cigarettes at the Grand Terrace club in Chicago. During the 1930s, I booked a big show for him in Detroit at a community center owned by the city, on Woodward and Garfield. The city rented the place out for concerts and other events. Since the place didn't have a bandstand, I hired some carpenters to build one. Billy performed on trumpet with a six- or seven-piece band. We had a sellout crowd.

In New York Joe and I went downtown to meet up with famous friends like Billy Eckstine and to mingle with the people. Walking along the street, I'd say to Joe, "Stop in here man, and say hello to the people." We knew a lot of places.

I always thought it was important that Joe stay in touch with the everyday folks. For instance, if an individual asked Joe for his autograph, I would tell him, "This young lady would like your autograph" and he would politely sign for her. So when we went into a place, be it New York or any big city, I often bought drinks for the people at the bar. Outside on the street, Joe would tell me, "Sunnie, you don't have to buy all those people drinks." I'd smile and simply tell him, "Don't worry about it. You cover the big ones, and I'll cover the little ones."

When Joe and I went to the Cotton Club, we never spent a dime. The owners were white gangsters from Chicago and they invited Joe to their place for publicity. I didn't think too much of the Cotton Club. Most everybody at the place was a thug or wanted to be a thug. I especially didn't like the control the management exerted over black performers.

I did, however, meet a nice young lady at the Cotton Club.

One day I took her to see my friend Louis Armstrong play. I had known Louis from his earlier visits to the Graystone Ballroom in Detroit. After the show, I asked her to dinner, but she explained that Louis had already promised to take her. Louis stole my gal and finally married her. But we always remained friends.

One evening I was sitting with Joe and Marva at a place and I talked them into walking over to the Nemo Club. When we got inside the club, I walked over to the headwaiter and said, "I'm Mr. Sunnie Wilson from Detroit. I want you to give all your waiters two dollars apiece. Give that emcee on the stage five dollars and tell him to come over and get my autograph during the break."

By this time Joe and Marva, without attracting notice, had taken their seats at a nearby table. Not long afterward, the waiters and the emcee came up to me and asked me for my autograph. The whole time Joe and Marva watched me and laughed because while the real celebrity sat unnoticed, I went around fooling these people into thinking I was the star.

Joe liked to play jokes on people, too. One time in St. Louis, Joe and I went to see Count Basie perform. Back at his hotel suite, Count showed us eight pairs of expensive shoes he had lying on the table. He just loved those fancy shoes. Without Count knowing it, Joe left the room with eight left shoes, leaving Count with eight right shoes. Next time I saw Count, he said, "Tell your friend Joe Louis to give me back my goddamn shoes!"

Joe could be funny, even at the expense of his own business ventures. When Joe was to appear on Gabriel Heatter's New York radio program, *We, The People*, he became very nervous about going on the air, so I went with him to the studio.

Gabriel Heatter possessed a deep and vibrant voice. On his show he featured guests of unusual talent, people who had achieved some special feat or status. On the night Joe appeared, two other guests were featured: the world's greatest hobo and the world's most laughing bartender. The hobo came on and told how he went around the world and never paid a fare and how he stowed in passage and sailed to countries all over the globe.

I stood in the wings as Joe approached the microphone with Gabriel Heatter. A nationally broadcast program, the show aired in front of a live audience. I could see Joe was uneasy. With a sudden burst, Gabriel Heatter announced: "Now, we have with us the greatest fighter in the world. Jack Johnson and Jack Dempsey never came near the greatness of my next guest. Let me introduce to you . . . The Brown Bomber . . . Mr. Joe Louis! Hello, Mr. Louis. You're still a fine-looking young man. Are you a Christian?"

"Yes sir," meekly answered Joe.

"Do you attend church?" inquired Heatter with the tone of a evangelist.

"Yes sir," again answered Joe.

"You never did drink?" continued Heatter.

"No sir."

"How many knockouts have you had?" asked Heatter.

"I just can't recall at the moment," returned Joe.

"Do you call your mother before every fight? What's her name?" Heatter continued.

"Miss Lillie, sir. And yes, I call her before every fight."

"Why do you call your mother?" he asked.

Joe answered calmly, "Because she prays for me."

"Well, I just think you're a wonderful young man. You're a model for all the children of America. Why don't you tell the kids out there what's your favorite soft drink."

Aware that Joe owned the Joe Louis Milk Company in Chicago and Joe Louis Punch, the producers and Gabriel Heatter saw a chance for Joe to promote his business ventures.

As the studio audience waited, Joe paused. Across America people sat by their radios to hear the Brown Bomber's reply. Joe's business partners could never had guessed the forthcoming answer. Everyone waited. Then he leaned toward the microphone and said, "Coca Cola." With these words, I imagined seeing his twenty-five-thousand-dollar share of Joe Louis Punch stock plunge.

On the way home from the studio, Joe and I didn't say a word until he broke the silence with, "I know I messed up." Not knowing whether to be mad or amused, I told him, "I didn't say anything," and returned to my silent demeanor. A little while later, feeling the weight of his conscience, he said, "I know I shouldn't have said Coke." Again I remained cold in my response: "I told you, I have not said a word about it." Later, I asked Joe how much Coca Cola had paid him to endorse their product. Joe must have drunk five or six Cokes a day. Sometimes Joe was just too damn honest.

During our trips to the West Coast, Joe and I often took the first-class train, the Santa Fe Super Chief. All the celebrities traveled on the Super Chief; sometimes we ran into Burt Lancaster and other Hollywood people. The train had luxurious sleeping cars, a bar, a dining car, a masseuse, a barber, and an in-house chef who would cook special meals for each guest. From the window of the train, I studied the various colors of the western terrain, the beautiful mountains, and the open sky. On the train you could relax and converse with passengers, play cards, or go back to bed. When Joe got to California he would attend private parties at people's homes, accompanied by celebrities like Jack Benny's sidekick, Eddie "Rochester" Anderson. Joe liked the company of Lena Horne. Despite the gossip about their intimacy, they remained good friends. Joe introduced Lena to a lot of important people and she remained grateful for Joe's help.

During the day, I would drive Joe to the golf course where he would play eighteen holes with Bob Hope or Bing Crosby at Lakeside Golf Course in North Hollywood, or anyone who would challenge him to a game. Sometimes after I picked Joe up, we drove over to Bing Crosby's live radio show. Bing often came straight from the golf course to do his show.

Mr. Roxborough and Joe's trainer, Jack Blackburn, opposed Joe's interest in golf. They believed it not only caused Joe to lose thousands of dollars, it disrupted his concentration on boxing. Nothing they said kept Joe from the game. He was addicted to the little white ball.

Although Joe looked upon the game as a form of release from his life as a celebrity, sometimes it caused him a great deal of frustration. During the late 1930s, Joe was not a very good golfer. On one occasion, when I picked Joe up from the golf course, he was standing near the curb without his bag and clubs. Later he told me he got mad and threw them across the fairway—

Joe didn't like to lose. When he became a decent player in later years, no one would play against him. By that time he had lost thousands of dollars on the golf course.

In California, Joe spent hours developing his golf game. On one occasion, Joe, Willie Adams, and I arrived in Los Angeles on the Super Chief and visited our friend Marshall Miles, whose wife had a place on Thirty-sixth Street. Marshall, a native of Buffalo, New York, became Joe's manager when Mr. Roxborough was sent to prison for numbers in 1942. Marshall's father owned a prosperous milk business. When he died, he left each of his four sons—Marshall, Mitchell, Dewey, and Percy—a fourth of his wealth. Mitchell Miles, the boss of the family, lived in Los Angeles, up the hill on Twenty-seventh Street, next door to the Japanese consul. On one of our visits to Los Angeles, I was carrying about three thousand dollars and Willie had about ten thousand; I don't know how much Marshall or Joe had, but they exceeded our amounts. Although Joe stayed at Marshall's and I shared a hotel room with Willie, we all put our money in Marshall's home safe.

The next day I drove Joe to the golf course. He played a golf game against a redcap, a porter he met who worked down at the airport. When we got ready to leave town, Willie, Marshall, and I went to the safe to get our money. After opening the door we couldn't believe it—there wasn't a dollar left. That damn redcap had beaten Joe and taken our money. We never saw a dime of it again.

Along with Joe's love for golf came an increasing interest in the art of horsemanship. Joe always loved horses. While out in California, he rode horses on a dude ranch. Back home he decided to acquire his own riding stables. He purchased a riding stable on a small farm in Shelby Township, Michigan, in 1938. In July of that year he held his first horse show, the U.S. Negro Horse Show. With Roxborough's backing, he purchased nearby Springhill Farm in Utica, Michigan, in 1939 for one hundred thousand dollars. Located on 440 acres, it was a beautiful place. The farm had a wooden, two-story farmhouse that Joe converted into a restaurant and cabaret. Once a stop on the Underground

Railroad, the house was built by a New York–born abolitionist farmer, Peter Lerich, a Methodist who, along with his wife Sarah, first built a log cabin on 220 acres in 1835. By the 1850s, the Lerichs expanded their ownership to 380 acres and dug a cave behind the house to hide slaves on their way to Marine City and Port Huron, where they crossed the river to Canada.

During the early years of Joe's ownership of the farm, I loved to drive out to Springhill, passing the rolling countryside and old graveyards surrounded by weeping willow trees. I was so impressed with the farm that I urged Mr. Roxborough to turn it into a resort to be called Joe Louisville. There was a flowing spring on the property and I told Mr. Roxborough that it would make an ideal place for building an apartment complex. He and his associates thought I was crazy. I also told him that the clear spring water could be bottled and sold, but he ignored my proposition. Instead, he opted to make a cabaret out of the farmhouse.

Roxborough also approved the building of a main horse stable, a circle track, bleachers for riding shows, and a dance pavilion with a capacity of fifteen hundred. Springhill stabled twenty-six school horses and twenty-four riding horses. For his personal use, Joe had five horses: Kentucky Rain, Clear Creek Prince, Freddy, Tiger Rose, and his favorite champion horse, Flash. Folks came out to rent horses and take riding lessons. Joe Louis was a hell of a rider. He could really make a horse gait.

One time, Joe decided to hold a horse show at Springhill and asked me to promote it. Sometimes I think Joe believed I possessed knowledge about everything. Although I informed him that I knew nothing about horses, he still urged me to promote the show. So I contacted a couple, the owners of a Detroit furniture store, who were experts in horsemanship, and they helped me locate the proper announcer and judges. The show brought in horses from all over the country, beautiful horses and ponies from Kentucky, Illinois, and Ohio. A large number of distinguished people turned out for the show. The events were divided between competitions for adult and children under eighteen. Judge Reuben Ray's daughter rode in the children's competition. It turned out to be a glamorous day.

Another time Joe called on me to promote a golf tournament for him at Rackham Municipal Golf Course in Huntington Woods, outside Detroit. I didn't know anything more about promoting a golf tournament than I did a horse show, but at least I knew a little about the sport. As a young man in Columbia, South Carolina, I worked at a golf course where the wealthy white folks played during the summer. These rich fellas called me by my childhood name, Little Willie. They'd be out there on the course nearly every day at daybreak, hitting balls and practicing. There weren't any caddies at this place. My job was to pick up the balls on the driving range.

Despite my efforts at Rackham, however, I didn't fare too well promoting the tournament. I lost three thousand dollars and Joe lost about four thousand gambling out on the course.

In 1942 Joe joined the army and spent his time fighting exhibition rounds for the troops. A year later, he, Sugar Ray Robinson, and I set out to make a little money. Initially, we sought to form a corporation to promote boxing fights and exhibitions. I planned to promote a fight with Sugar Ray Robinson featuring Joe as referee. With two stars in the ring, I hoped to pack the house. But unknown to me, Ray Robinson and Nick Londos, the promoter for Olympia Stadium,[4] had made a deal behind my back. One day I looked up at a big sign that read, "Sugar Ray Robinson versus Jake Lamotta at Olympia Stadium." Scheduled for February 1943, it was the first rematch between Ray and Lamotta, the Raging Bull, since Ray had beaten Lamotta in New York several months earlier. I attended the fight, but I was mad as hell. Jake whipped Ray. I didn't talk to Ray for a long time. Later he apologized, explaining that his manager organized the fight without his knowledge.

Since Mr. Roxborough took all my good fighters, I eventually turned in my license. I just didn't have his kind of money. Mr.

---

4. Opened in 1927 at 5920 W. Grand Boulevard as the largest indoor ice arena in the world, Olympia Sports Arena was the home of the Detroit Red Wings and hosted many other sports and entertainment events. The Olympia closed in 1979 and was demolished in 1986. The Red Wings' current home, located on the city's waterfront, was christened Joe Louis Arena in honor of Detroit's hometown boxing champion.

Roxborough was the boss. He wanted nothing bad connected with Joe. "Keep him clean!" he commanded. "Keep him out of bad places and don't let him get hooked with bad people." We kept a good image because Joe was our meal ticket. There are no bad pictures of Joe because we didn't allow any to be taken. Freddie Guinyard, Freddie Wilson, a heavyweight prizefighter, and I knocked down more cameramen and reporters than Joe did opponents in the ring. They followed Joe around to dig up dirt on him, so we cracked them upside the head. Joe played around. He was human like everybody else. But it's not how much you play; it's how much people know you play. Joe was always a gentleman.

Although many believed Joe to be uneducated, they didn't know that he had his own tutor, Russell Cowans, who accompanied him along with his private physician and chef Bill Bottoms. A black sports journalist and photographer with the *Detroit Tribune,* Cowans graduated with a master's degree from the University of Michigan. He assisted Joe in completing his high-school education. Hired in 1935, Cowans spent two hours daily helping Joe with his studies in liberal arts and math. As far as I'm concerned Joe earned his Ph.D.—the Golden Gloves was his master's degree and the world championship his doctorate.

With his dignified public image, Joe was constantly called on to attend public events. In 1947 Joe and I attended a ceremony in Baltimore that dedicated a recreational center to our old friend, Chick Webb, one the greatest drummers and showmen I had ever known. The dedication drew the likes of labor leader A. Philip Randolph, Maryland governor O'Connor, and journalist Billy Rowe. A quiet individual, Chick was a hunchbacked little man. I first met him in the mid-1930s backstage at the Paradise Theater. Chick was one my few friends, including trumpeter Freddie Jenkins, whom I found to be shorter than myself. I often saw him perform at the Savoy Ballroom in Harlem. Sometimes the hump on his back would burst open, causing him tremendous pain. Though he suffered from tuberculosis of the spine, Chick performed up until the day he died in June 1939. His motto was, "The show must go on." If there was anyone who epitomized that saying, it was Chick Webb. The dedication was a beautiful tribute; the words of the speakers nearly brought tears to my eyes.

That same year, on June 24, Joe and I went to Cleveland to watch Sugar Ray fight Jimmy Doyle. Though I had not talked to Ray since our falling out over the Lamotta fight at the Olympia, Joe had remained close to him. I held a grudge. We watched Ray knock out Doyle. Taking a left hook from Ray in the eighth round, Doyle fell, hitting his head on the canvas. The attendants came and took out Doyle by stretcher. No one knew the seriousness of Doyle's condition, that he would never regain consciousness. That's the brutal nature of boxing. A fighter may be knocked out or be left with a serious injury. Boxing is a hard business and a bull's game. Sugar Ray gave half his earnings from a later fight to Doyle's mother.

In December 1947 I went to New York City to watch Joe fight Jersey Joe Walcott at Madison Square Garden. Before the fight, I warned Joe not to fight Walcott. Joe wanted to help Walcott make a little money. Walcott had been Joe's sparring partner during the first Schmeling-Louis fight in 1936. He had a nice family, and Joe was a kind-hearted man, so he agreed to help Walcott make a few bucks by fighting an exhibition, something Joe did for many poor fighters. Back then, if you knocked out the champion in an exhibition fight, you won the title. I don't think Joe took the Walcott fight very seriously. He didn't train much for it. He didn't want to hurt his sparring partner.

But Joe's old sparring partner sure managed to hurt him. As his sparring partner, Walcott knew all of Joe's moves and timing. He was no second-rate fighter. He had once trained under Joe's trainer, Jack Blackburn. He was mean in the ring. From my seat at the fight, I yelled out to Joe, "Move in, champ; keep your left hand down . . . come on, goddamn it!"

When you're sitting ringside with your fighter's entourage—the doctor, managers, and so forth—there are strict rules and regulations against talking or communicating with your boxer. It can penalize the fighter. The trainer is the only one who has the right to communicate with the fighter. You can be five rows back in the audience yelling anything you want, but not ringside. I had no business interfering. Since I was shouting out commands

97

to Joe, the officials sent some security men to escort me out into the hallway. Without a word, these two big fellas grabbed me by each arm, lifted me from my seat, and carried me away. As the security men and I made our way through the crowd, I looked up and saw Ray Robinson laughing at me. I had to watch the rest of the fight from the turnstile.

Walcott gave Joe fierce competition. He knocked Joe down in the first and fourth rounds, hitting him with well-landed blows that closed up Joe's left eye. After fifteen rounds, referee Ruby Goldstein voted for Walcott, but the judges unanimously cast their votes with Joe. Though Joe won by decision, Walcott beat him good. Josephine Baker, one of the celebrities to attend the bout, approached me after the fight, tears flowing from her eyes. I asked her, "What you crying for? The boy didn't lose yet." It was odd to see Ms. Baker carrying on like that, because she was a strong-willed and dignified woman.

I blamed Joe's near defeat on his management. When someone manages a celebrity, whether a musician or a sports figure, he must think of that individual's well-being and how a decision or an event will affect the future of his career. As a manager you are paid to protect a person's interests. The Walcott fight was an example of how a lack of foresight and greed can jeopardize a celebrity's career.

Joe didn't like the idea of being bested in the ring. As with all of Joe's fights, we had planned a big victory party in the hotel, one that attracted show people like Cab Calloway and other celebrities. Renting out an entire floor, we had pretty women and tables set up with champagne, whiskey, beer, and food. After the fight, everybody was waiting, but Joe never showed. We got word that Joe wasn't coming. So I said, "What the hell, let's go ahead and eat anyway." I let it become my party instead.

Joe was a hard loser. He liked to dish out punishment, but he didn't like to take it. I believe he always had a fear of losing. A day and a half later, I tracked Joe down at his room on St. Nicholas Place. Angered by his down-and-out attitude, I said, "Everybody was waiting for you, Joe. We had champagne and pretty girls and you let us all down. Then I find you here all alone. You are certainly a sore loser, especially after you've have knocked down and hurt so many young men. You have no right to sit here and feel sorry for yourself. Damn Walcott, you can show him up the next time." He stood there and somberly replied, "You're right." I said, "Let's go out and have a drink." Joe put on his jacket and we went downtown.

In 1941 I purchased the Forest Club at Forest and Hastings. With a roller rink, meeting hall, and bowling alley the Forest Club was larger than the old Madison Square Garden.

The 107-foot bar in the Forest Club was the "longest bar in town."

With my daughter Sharon at the Forest Club.

Advertisement for
Forest Club opening.

The Forest Club's vault, "The Celebrity Room," served as my private meeting spot where I entertained special guests. Here I'm spending some time with jazz pianist Earl Hines.

Toasting my good friend Lionel Hampton (c. 1940s).

The Forest Club's skating teams competed at rinks all over the Midwest.

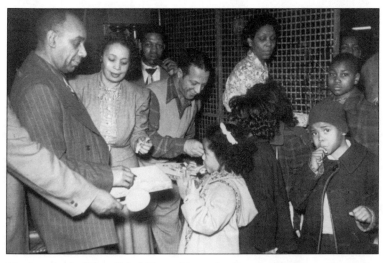

During the holidays I held benefit parties for the black youngsters in the Forest Club's roller rink.

SUNNIE WILSON'S
SHOW · BAR

proudly presents

Clarence "Gatemouth" Brown
The man from Texas Bringing
the Blues

★ Tina Dixon

The Great Sandra
"Exotic Dancer"

and as

M C.—Host—Producer

JOE "ZIGGY" JOHNSON

Visit Ziggy's
Blue Room

GATEMOUTH

FOREST and HASTINGS

In 1951 I brought my friend and talented show producer Joe Ziggy into the Forest Club, and provided him with a new in-house venue, "Ziggy's Blue Room."

Sitting on the steps of the Mark Twain Hotel on Garfield just off
Woodward Avenue.

Having a champagne birthday celebration at the Mark Twain Hotel
(c. 1950s).

Idlewild island was originally connected to the mainland by a log auto bridge. (Courtesy State Archives of Michigan.)

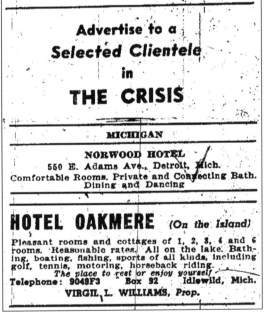

As one of the leading black resorts in America, Idlewild was regularly advertised, throughout the 1930s, in the NAACP's periodical, *The Crisis.*

A bring-your-own establishment, the Wilsons' Purple Palace was one of Idlewild's early night spots. (Courtesy State Archives of Michigan.)

The Paradise became the first nightclub to open in the area, and over the years it remained the premier place for entertainment. (Courtesy State Archives of Michigan.)

The El Morocco, owned by Raja, served as Idlewild's after-hours drinking and dining spot. (Courtesy Burton Historical Collection.)

With friends in good old Idlewild.

I took Joe Louis up to Idlewild. Afterward, he
became a frequent guest.

Mr. Williams, a Chicago theater owner, and his wife, Virgil Williams. Mr. Williams was one of the founders of Idlewild (c. 1940s).

More friends in Idlewild.

Idlewild Beach is one of two public beaches in Yates County. (Photo by Gretta Abu-Isa.)

In 1952 I helped found the Detroit Idlewilders Club and served as its first president.

Advertisement for Arthur Braggs's Idlewild Revue.

◆ 5 ◆
Down on Hastings Street

Forest and Hastings!
Sunnie Wilson,
longest bar in town.
That's the onlyst bar you can walk in
when you get ready to buy a bottle beer
you have to walk a mile after you get in the joint
—Detroit Count, 1948[1]

Since the turn of the century, Hastings Street remained the main economic lifeline of the black and Jewish east-side communities. Extending north beyond the Paradise Valley black-owned entertainment spots on Adams and St. Antoine, Hastings possessed a distinct history and character that earned it a far different image and worldwide reputation. Though Adams and St. Antoine competed for the title of the Broadway of Paradise Valley, Hastings emerged in the first decades of the twentieth century primarily as a business thoroughfare occupied by a diverse ethnic population.

In the late 1800s the drivers of horses along Hastings' sixty-block stretch encountered a rough stone surface between Atwater

---

1. "Hastings Street Opera, Part I," recorded on Joseph Von Battle's JVB label in 1948 by Detroit Count (Bob White), became a local hit.

101

and Jefferson, which changed to brick between Jefferson and Mullet. On Jefferson and Hastings, Detroiters of genteel background visited the Detroit Museum of Art. North of the Jewish district between Mullet and Grand Boulevard existed a cruder section paved with dirt and cedar. In this area of Hastings, blacks opened several small businesses.

After 1900 black, middle-class newcomers from the South contributed to the economic development of the east-side ghetto. Their aggressiveness and determination to achieve economic success in the North led to a transformation in the appearance of streets like St. Antoine and Hastings. Throughout the east side, blacks opened drugstores, funeral parlors, lumberyards, cigar stands, and saloons. Soon the area bound by St. Antoine and Hastings became a thriving center for gambling joints, nightclubs, and illicit sporting houses.

Over the next three decades, Hastings emerged as the east side's center for black business. Through the funds acquired by gambling or money borrowed from loan sharks, blacks established a number of small businesses on Hastings. Paying as much as 50 percent interest to loan sharks, these businessmen opened barbershops, newspaper stands, and shoe-shine parlors. Black-owned shrimp huts sprang up on nearly every corner, filling the neighborhood with a thick, spicy smoke that hung in the air for blocks.

Small, black enterprises arising out of the underground economy existed side by side with businesses of middle-class entrepreneurs who opened their own tailor shops, groceries, and fish markets financed by bank loans and personal savings. Educated black professionals along Hastings established a number of private medical practices, including J. W. Collins, who specialized in "painless extractions," and Dr. C. C. Strickland, who treated "private diseases." Sidney Barthwell, one of the most famous east-side businessmen, opened a chain of nine drugstores, one of which was on Hastings. Attesting to the economic vitality of the street, Sunnie Wilson's former nightclub employer, Mac Ivey, related, "Hastings Street always struck me as a good place to do business . . . always alive, and folks on it like to spend money and have a good time."

Launching his legendary entertainment center, the Forest Club, on Hastings in 1941, Wilson joined the city's pioneer black businessmen in establishing the street as a thriving center for trade and nightlife. As owner of the Forest Club, Wilson rented his hall to various individuals and organizations, including the Homer Martin–led American Federation of Labor (AFL) when it battled for union recognition during the 1941 River Rouge strike.

During the height of the cold war, Wilson agreed, amid opposition from the Detroit Police Department and city hall, to allow singer and Communist activist Paul Robeson to appear at his club. Just five months after the end of Stalin's Berlin blockade and during the founding of the People's Republic of China, Robeson embarked on a nationwide tour to defend eleven prominent American Communists indicted by the federal government. Robeson's appearances caused a wave of anti-Communist protest from veterans' groups, police, and members of city hall. Taking the stage at the Forest Club, on October 9, 1949, Robeson asked the crowd, "What has happened? I'm still the same man." Turned away by many of his previous supporters, he lamented, "I still speak and fight for justice, against fascism, for peace, like I did in those days. Just what has happened is that I'm fighting for it now, that's why the atmosphere has changed."[2] Influenced by events of the cold war, many no longer viewed Robeson as the champion of labor and antifascism, but as the voice of Red Communism threatening American democracy. One of Robeson's biographers later wrote that October 1949 "was a tense time; word was out that to hold a Paul Robeson concert meant to invite a riot."[3]

Undaunted by death threats and public criticism, Wilson allowed Robeson to appear at his club. Erma Henderson, founder of the Detroit Committee to Welcome Robeson, recalled Wilson's generosity in offering his hall to Robeson. "We visited my dear friend, Sunnie Wilson, who owned the famous Forest Club. . . . Although Sunnie Wilson was young, he was one of the most influential and

---

2. Phillip S. Foner, ed., *Paul Robeson Speaks: Writings, Speeches, Interviews, 1918–1974* (New York: Citadel Press, 1978), 233–34. Excerpts from the Forest Club speech titled "I Am the Same Man," which originally appeared in the *Daily Worker,* October 12, 1949.

3. Dorothy Butler Gilliam, *Paul Robeson: All American* (Washington, D.C.: New Republic Books, 1978), 156.

*successful African American business leaders in the city of Detroit
and the State of Michigan. He agreed to allow Robeson to be scheduled at the Forest Club.*"[4] *In charge of security for the appearance,
Coleman A. Young lauded Wilson's willingness to secure his hall for
the renowned Robeson as his "most glorious moment."*[5]

After all the excitement and glamor had waned at the Brown
Bomber's Chicken Shack, I began to search for new horizons. A
gentleman named Reverend Otis came to see me and told of a
place for rent on Hastings. Located on the corner of Forest and
Hastings, the Forest Club ran an entire block. It was bigger than
Madison Square Garden. In the twenties the building had been
an indoor amusement park. The Forest Club had a banquet hall,
dance floor, a two-level roller-skating rink, and twenty-six lanes
for bowling. The club had three white owners, one of whom was
my friend Leo Adler, a wealthy white businessman who loaned
me twenty-five thousand dollars to buy out the lease. Mr. Adler
came from a monied family. He owned the Bowl-O-Drome on
Dexter. Years later, Mr. Adler opened a car dealership and co-
owned The Flagpole restaurant on Livernois.

Though Hastings remained a center of Jewish business, I
joined several other black entrepreneurs in conducting business
along the avenue. On Willis and Hastings Mr. Turner had a very
prosperous grocery store. The McFall Brothers—Benjamin,
George, and James—from Valdosta, Georgia, operated a successful funeral home at 714 E. Canfield and Hastings, and at 3007
Hastings near Forest, Mrs. Vivian Nash ran a black beauty school.
In the same building a West Indian physician, Dr. J. C. Randolpho, had an office. The city employed Dr. Randolpho to look
after the health of its black police officers. An honest man, Dr.

---

4. Elaine Latzman Moon, *Untold Tales, Unsung Heroes: An Oral
History of Detroit's African-American Community, 1918–1967* (Detroit:
Wayne State University Press, 1994), 196.
5. Kathy Jackson, "Sunnie Rising Again? Benefit Will Aid
Innkeeper Who Brought Stars to Detroit," *Crain's Detroit Business,*
August 17, 1987, 28.

Randolpho, after diagnosing your illness, would work out a flat rate for your recovery.

The only black-owned nightclub on Hastings during the 1930s was Mac Ivey's Cozy Corner. My acquiring the Forest Club upset my white competitors who owned established bars on adjacent corners. In an effort to block my purchase, the local businessmen signed petitions in protest against me. I told my friend Police Inspector Edwin Morgan about the situation and he told me to move in at night. Down through the years, Inspector Morgan gave me valuable advice. Back when I got into some trouble working for Sammy Brandt, he encouraged me to go into business for myself. A big-framed man who spoke with a heavy brogue, Inspector Morgan hailed from County Cork, Ireland. He was the greatest man ever to wear a uniform. He showed the same respect for blacks as he did for the whites. In my years on the east side, he was the only white policeman I knew who walked alone, without bodyguards, through the Negro neighborhood.

Morgan left Ireland and arrived in America at age seventeen. He fought in France in World War I and earned a Purple Heart and the Silver Star for bravery. After joining the police force in 1922, he worked out of the Thirteenth Precinct on the clean-up squad, riding on the Black Maria, the police wagon that transported prisoners. He would stand on the running board to keep the prisoners inside the paddy wagon. Back then they didn't handcuff or chain you. They just shoved you inside the wagon, and the officers would stand guard outside. He told me that he never arrested a man without warning him first. If he knocked on your door on Friday and warned you to be out by Monday, he meant it. If you were still there on Monday, he kicked the door in. With the support of Inspector Morgan, who sent a squad car to accompany me, I moved in late at night.

When my competition woke the next morning, they found the Forest Club occupied by Sunnie Wilson. My purchase of the Forest Club drew me into a new field of enterprise, which had been owned by the white business world, particularly the Jewish businessmen who, since the turn of the century, owned the larger business operations on Hastings: bars, restaurants, and apartment buildings. As I have pointed out, Mac Ivey's Cozy Corner was the only black-owned bar on Hastings. At that time most black-owned businesses in Paradise Valley were barbershops, shoe-shine parlors, and fish markets.

My first weeks of business were made difficult by vindictive white customers who poured ammonia on the floor and lit stink bombs in the bar. I contacted Joe Louis and told him that because of this harassment, I couldn't make any money. He sent the Brown Bomber softball team to the bar. Most of Joe's associates could fight. Whenever my boys caught one of these troublemakers, they escorted him to Jake's Bar across the street and threw him right into the door. Another time they took a fella and threw him through the door of Mary's Bar down the way, with the message that if it happened again, they'd come get the owner. I knew who the real troublemakers were, and I sent them all the same message: "I'm here to stay!"

Soon business got good, and I paid off all my debts at the Chicken Shack. Because the club was located at a streetcar stop, my business benefitted from the steady flow of people arriving and departing from the street. When the conductor let off passengers outside my place he shouted: "Last stop, Sunnie's Corner!" Soon the intersection became known as "Sunnie's Corner." I put up a big sign outside my place reading, "Stop in and Get Your Morning Nip." Everybody came to my club—the blacks, the whites, the famous and not-so-famous. My patrons from the Chicken Shack followed me.[6]

As a result of the expansion of my club, I hired nearly three hundred employees, including clerks, bartenders, cooks, waiters, and bouncers. I ran the Forest Club as a tight operation. My floor men carried no guns or blackjacks. With the exception of one individual, they were all ex-heavyweight prizefighters—professionals who knew how to maintain order. Among them was Clin-

---

6. Ulysses Boykin wrote in two articles, both titled "Jumpin' Jive" for the *Detroit Tribune*, "Wilson's new spot . . . the Cocktail Bar and Lounge of the Forest Club is the place to take your friends" (February 15, 1941, p. 10), and "Wilson's new cocktail bar on Forest is jumpin'!" (March 1, 1941, p. 8).

ton Bridges, a big, tough prizefighter. Back in the early 1930s, Clinton had been intercity lightweight Golden Gloves champ. In an early amateur bout he out-pointed Joe Louis.

One night while dealing with a drunken troublemaker at the end of the bar, I called Clinton to keep an eye on him until the police arrived. Because some of my patrons didn't like white folks, especially white policemen, I didn't let the officers arrest anybody unless they were accompanied by one of my bouncers. This particular evening, the police walked up along the bar with Clinton. The fella wasn't going to give in easy. He grabbed a bottle and cracked the end of it over the bar, using its sharp, jagged edge to hold off the officers. Clinton walked up and, standing less than an arm's-length away, hit the man with one solid blow, knocking him to the floor. "Now clean up that mess you made," ordered Clinton. On his hands and knees the dazed troublemaker began to pick up all the broken shards of glass. Because of the order I kept, police chiefs and other law enforcement people came to the bar to study mob control.

After establishing order in the club, I made plans to extend my original 37-foot bar to 107 feet. I set a date for the opening of my new custom bar, the longest in the state of Michigan, longer than the Brass Rail. To have it installed I needed thirteen thousand dollars. I called Cab Calloway to ask for some money, but he told me the race track took his pocket change. I had very good credit with my bank. Because I had a white accountant who handled my finances, I never made personal trips to the bank. All I knew was the Brinks armored-car driver who came to pick up my money.

To secure a loan for the remodeling of my bar, I made a date with the bank's vice president. He praised me for having a fine account. He asked me what I wanted the loan for, and I told him I wanted to remodel my bar.

As I sat before the vice president and two other white men, he said, "Mr. Wilson, I'm sorry but our bank cannot finance a bar, because if you default on your payments we have no means to run such a business." "You mean to tell me," I responded, "that you have my money in your bank and you cannot give a loan? I guess I'll have to take my money elsewhere."

I went to a number of banks and received the same story. I became very disgusted. Then I talked to fellow bar owner Grady Jackson. He said, "What you worrying about, man? Go up and see Mr. Katz on Woodward Avenue." So I went to Mr. Katz's office. When I walked through the door, he greeted me. "Mr. Wilson, I've heard so much about you. How can I help you?" "I'm planning to open my new bar over on Hastings in a week, and I need some money," I said. "How much?" he inquired. "About thirteen thousand dollars," I answered.

To my surprise, he then offered me fifteen thousand dollars. He called the cabinet company and instructed them to build my bar. I never signed a contract, not one paper. The next thing I knew, my place swarmed with electricians, plumbers, and cabinet makers. Eventually I built a stage on my dance floor that accommodated seven hundred dancers and began to hire big bands.

Several years before I bought the Forest Club, I had promoted shows in the club's ballroom. A partner and I rented the club's ballroom and brought in pianist Fats Waller. At that time we could afford to hire Fats, because he wasn't doing so well financially. Like most bandleaders during those days, Fats Waller didn't travel with his entire band. He brought only his bass player. He rode by car all the way from St. Louis, sitting behind the big bass fiddle. When he got to Detroit, he hired local musicians to fill out his group. The night of the show, despite cold weather, the place was packed. Charging one dollar at the door, my partner and I made thirty-five hundred dollars. With the success of the show, Fats and I became good friends. A natural-born comedian, Fats was my man.

Following the purchase of the club, I brought in a number of national acts like Louis Jordan, Jay McShann, Eddie Durham, Al Hibbler, Charlie Parker, and Dizzy Gillespie. I brought in the Nat King Cole Trio for its first appearance in Detroit. Traveling in California, Joe Louis and I walked into the Trocadero Club in Hollywood where Nat King Cole had his own room, the Nat King Cole Room—a cabaret where you were required to wear a suit and tie. The Nat King Cole Room featured the Nat King Cole Trio. I was so impressed with Nat's group that I asked him if he wanted to perform at my place. A couple of months later he appeared for two weekends at the Forest Club. He packed the place.

With its offering of entertainment and the genial atmosphere, the Forest Club became a gathering spot for famous musicians and entertainers. My customers were thrilled to meet celebrities like Cab Calloway, Earl Hines, and Lionel Hampton, who came in after their shows at the Graystone Ballroom and Paradise Theater. These big-name performers never spent a dime in my place. They were my special guests.

Lionel Hampton was a regular at the club. Everybody called him Gates. He married a sharp business woman, Gladys Riddle, who controlled Lionel's financial assets. Three years older than Lionel, Gladys was a beautiful, light-skinned woman who had attended Fisk University in Nashville. She was a tough individual. The only time I saw her show emotion was when her little dog ran out in the street and got hit by a car. She stood over the dog, pleading, "God, don't let him die." The dog died, and she broke into tears. As Lionel once said, "She was the boss off-stage, and I was the boss on-stage." Lionel owned a tour bus and a Cadillac. He rode in the bus with the band, and Gladys rode in the Cadillac.

But Gladys was Lionel's soul mate. She looked out for his future. "Mr. Wilson," she said, "a lot of musicians and celebrities, after reaching stardom and making a tremendous amounts of money, die broke. But Lionel will never die broke or have to depend on others to support him because I'm preparing everything for my dear husband. If I were to pass away and not have his financial well-being in order, I would never be able to rest in the great beyond." Some thirty years later, Gladys died of a heart attack. Though her death nearly devastated Lionel, today he is a wealthy man due to the hard work and commitment of his devoted wife.

After one of his shows, Lionel came into my place and asked if I wanted to go to Olympia Stadium to see a prizefight. Gladys asked me, "How much money should I give him?" I answered, "One hundred dollars." "Oh no, he's not going to spend a hundred dollars of my money!" She finally gave him seventy-five dollars and I covered the rest of his tab.

But I didn't acquire the Forest Club just to book entertainment and socialize with celebrities. In the club we set up a school for poor black people to learn to read and write. Watching these women and men learning to write their names was an emotionally moving experience. They had tears running down their cheeks. Volunteer instructors from the black sororities taught the women how to sit and walk like ladies. Students learned by watching and emulating the teacher. Eventually, the women formed two sororities.

Like most of the black businessmen in Paradise Valley, I put money back into the community. At the Forest Club I sponsored annual Christmas and Thanksgiving parties which drew thousands of people. I called upon local businessmen to contribute something to the event. One store might send a bushel of apples, another articles of clothing. I accepted no checks or cash, just merchandise that could be distributed to the children. Booking agent Chester Rentie and local nightclubs such as the Parrot Lounge, Frolic Show Bar, Lee's Sensation, and the El Sino contributed entertainment.

I held my annual Christmas party in the Forest Club roller rink. My associates and I handed out candy canes and fruit to the children. We gave presents—bicycles, tricycles, and the like. We also gave out baskets of fruit to the poor. During one of our parties, nearly one thousand children, ranging in age from four to fourteen, consumed one thousand hot dogs and seventy-five cases of soda pop. On Easter Sunday we organized egg hunts for the kids. The white bar owners on the street protested my holding these events and forced me to appear before the Liquor Control Commission. When you hold a bar license, you're not supposed to solicit other businesses. The annual parties were eventually held at the Graystone Ballroom.

On the weekends the school kids lined up to get in the Forest Club's roller-skating rink, advertised as the "World's Largest Race Owned and Operated Roller Skating Rink."[7] As a member

---

7. Isaac Jones, "Hastings after Dark," *Michigan Chronicle*, August 6, 1949, p. 23. Jones writes: "inside a huge building at Forest and Hastings the young people are burning the floor with roller skates."

of the National Roller Rink Operators Association, I hired women managers, making me one of the first businessmen in the city to stress the employment of black women in supervisory positions. The rink featured many talented skaters who belonged to the Regent Figure Skating Club.

We never had any trouble at the rink. I took the bad children of the neighborhood and gave them jobs keeping order at the skating rink. I would say, "Come here, boys, you sell tickets today, and you collect skates, and you be the floor man." The rink had two levels: the main floor for the experienced skaters and an upper area for the beginners. Our freestyle and speed skaters competed in national championships held at the Pla-Mor Roller Rink in Cleveland and the Park City Bowl in Chicago.

As owner of the Forest Club, I got involved in many important events. In April 1941 I rented the club to the AFL, when strikers shut down the River Rouge plant. Ford employed nearly fourteen thousand black workers, more than any other industrial company in the world. About one-sixth of this number worked at the Rouge plant. To gain their support in the upcoming National Labor Relations Board election, the UAW-CIO and the Ford-backed UAW-AFL both bid for the workers' recognition. On April 2, the second night of the strike, the AFL held back-to-work meetings in the black neighborhood, including one at my place. On the night of the meeting, two thousand workers jammed my hall. In an effort to deter an outbreak of violence, my friend Inspector Morgan placed policemen around the club. The AFL expected a fight with outside agitators. Union members brought in sticks and clubs. I didn't fear anything because these people were fighting for a cause. Although there was no violence, the next day I found their makeshift weapons lying all over my meeting hall.[8]

During this time, I also set out to help the black community

---

8. "More than 2,000 attended the meeting at the Forest Club, while approximately 100 were not able to gain admittance to the building. Police under Inspector Edward [sic] Morgan of Canfield Station, were stationed at the building to avoid trouble." Bill Lane, "Strong Pleas Made by Both CIO and AFL," *Detroit Tribune,* April 5, 1941, p. 1.

and traveling entertainers by purchasing the Mark Twain Hotel in 1943. At that time blacks couldn't stay in white hotels. So I bought one. I originally went to New York to buy the Theresa located on 125th Street in Harlem, but when the owners found out that Joe Louis was my partner, they raised the price from $350,000 to $500,000. I was walking around New York with $150,000 in checks in my pocket. I gave them to the owners and then called Joe to ask him for $50,000 more. When I told him I wanted to buy the Theresa, he just laughed. He knew I was in way over my head.

Instead, I went back to Detroit and opened the Mark Twain, a three-story, sixty-two-room hotel on Garfield just off of Woodward Avenue. Every room had a private bath and a telephone. I had maid service and waiters who would bring the guests anything they wanted to eat or drink. Though there were other larger black-owned hotels in Detroit, like the Gotham and Carlton Plaza, they charged high prices that many musicians could not afford. Nobody went hungry at my hotel. If the entertainers were broke, they stayed whether they had money or not. The musicians were my guests.

The top floor of the Mark Twain had a private meeting room, a beautifully decorated place with reclining chairs and a bar where I entertained my guests. Duke Ellington nicknamed it the Top of the Mark. All the musicians used that room. Singer Betty Carter threw a party at the Top of the Mark for Ray Charles and his group. If my musician friends wanted to jam they'd go downstairs to the lounge; if they wanted to relax I'd invite them to the Top of the Mark.

Many of the big names stayed at the Mark Twain: Lionel Hampton, Cootie Williams, Chico Hamilton, Arthur Prysock, and Gene "Red Top" Ammons, who eventually married one of my maids. He wrote his hit "Red Top" about her and her red hair. Count Basie loved to stay at the Mark Twain and everybody at the hotel loved him. I was a little closer to Count than to Duke. Like my friend Cab Calloway, Count liked to play the horses. Count's manager asked me to have a talk with Count about his race-track problem. Eventually, his manager put him on a restricted weekly salary.

112

All the musicians fought for the use of Suite Fifty. The musicians called it the lucky suite. Suite Fifty gained a reputation because whenever an entertainer checked into the room, he landed high-paying jobs from booking agents. When Billy Eckstine stayed in Suite Fifty he got $450 from a show, and later Sarah Vaughan got $500.

In my first years on Hastings, I encountered only one mildly dangerous incident. One night when I let the help close the club, I went to the Willis Theater on Hastings to catch a Tom Mix picture. Looking up at the screen, I saw Tom and his buddy confronted by two outlaws. When Tom's sidekick discovered the outlaws hiding behind a door, he yelled, "Look behind you, Tom!" Just when Tom pulled the trigger, someone in the audience fired a shot that put a big hole in the screen. People started screaming and running out of the place. I ducked down between the seats and didn't come up until the place was empty.

Although I had known no serious violence on the east side, events would soon culminate in one of the worst urban riots of the war years. On June 20, 1943, Hastings became the site of the Detroit riot—three days of violence and destruction. That afternoon about one hundred thousand people crowded on Belle Isle. While crossing the bridge back to the city, two young black men attempted to throw a man off the bridge, causing white sailors to attack these two black youngsters.

Later that evening, by the time the police had broken up the crowds on Jefferson Avenue, seven hundred dancers crowded the Forest Club's ballroom. Though I did not witness the event, they tell me that a young black man named Leo Tipton came into my place. Dressed in a suit and carrying a briefcase, he jumped onto the stage, grabbed the microphone, and announced that a black woman and her baby had been thrown off the Belle Isle Bridge. He told the crowd that cars were waiting outside to take them downtown. Incited by Tipton's announcement, the crowd rushed out the door onto Hastings. After the crowd discovered the street was empty and that Tipton had lied about the cars waiting to take them downtown, people began to throw rocks at passing white motorists and at the windows of the Jewish stores. Though I was at the club that night, I did not witness the entrance of Leo Tipton. Many sources claim that Tipton worked at the Forest Club, but I do not remember him ever working for me.

The riot wasn't about the troublesome crowds on Belle Isle or the rumors spread by Leo Tipton; it was about the brutality of the Detroit Police Department. Traditionally, the police had always been cruel in their treatment of Detroit's black folks. Racial animosity within the police department emerged out of a leftover Southern hatred for blacks. These patrolmen, many of them Southern born, were raised on hatred for black people and they fought to maintain a sense of superiority. With all the racial hatred, violent confrontation was imminent. Before the riot, the bluecoats' pent-up animosity usually showed itself when these officers hit some Negro in the head with their billy clubs.

Blind power is often rudely awakened. I had observed trouble brewing on the streets for years. One evening, not long after my purchase of the Forest Club, two black women got in a fight outside my place. Called to the scene, two white officers came into my club. They asked me, aware of my reputation with the black folks of the neighborhood, if I would help settle the dispute. Walking outside, I saw the two women sitting in the patrol car. Approaching the car, I stopped and asked the officers, "Gentlemen, can I have a word with you?" They agreed. I told them, "There is a lot of tension here tonight. I'm not telling you what to do, but it would be better if you'd either take these ladies home or lock them up." "Goddamn you!" snapped one of the officers. "I'll lock them up and you, too." "Go right ahead," I said.

They put me in the car and took us to Canfield Street Station. Inside, a lieutenant addressed me, "Mr. Wilson, I have some advice for you. You run that goddamned bar and let us run the police station." I responded, "Sir, I want to let you know that about three hundred people have followed the patrol car from the Forest Club and are standing outside to protest my arrest." A few hours later, I was released. The next day, I was called down to the station by Inspector Morgan, who sent for the lieutenant. "This man's name is Mr. Wilson," admonished Morgan. "Do you understand?" "Yes sir," answered the lieutenant, uncomfortably swallowing his pride.

114

I reminded the lieutenant that if relations didn't improve the city was headed toward a race riot. You could feel the tension in the air, and what occurred on the June 20 could have happened anywhere in the city. Any incident could have provided the spark.

Looking back, there were many officers I didn't like and some I did, especially my friend Inspector Morgan. Many of the officers respected me and I respected them. When I owned the Chicken Shack, I called the officers to my back door, where I gave them free chicken and whiskey. Sometimes, when these fellas were drinking at the back door, an officer would show up in the bar looking for the drivers of the empty patrol cars parked out front. To help these patrolmen, I would hide them in the basement of the Chicken Shack until their commanding officer left the building. When I went out of town, these policemen would watch my apartment across the street on Vernor. I had no problem with the police.

During the first night of the riot, however, these same policemen, some of whom I had fed and looked after, broke into my apartment. When I got to my building, every door in the place had been kicked in. At my place I had a beautiful wine collection. My friends Mr. and Mrs. McDonald, owners of the McDonald Wine Company, taught me about champagne and fine wine. When they visited Europe, the McDonalds brought me expensive crème de menthe and rare wines dating back a hundred years. Since I didn't have a basement for a wine cellar, I built a shelf for all my fine wines. Entering my place, I found my clothes strewn around the room, my piano in the den hacked-up by axes, and my nice wine collection nothing more that broken bottles and stains on the floor. They couldn't have been searching for weapons because my gold derringer pistol was still in the desk drawer. My rings and other expensive belongings had been stolen.

With my place in shambles, I spent the evening in the Forest Club. Instructing my employees to go home to their families, I remained alone, except for my dog. Small and muscular, the dog had short, white hair, the kind that you could see through to the pinkish color of its skin. Holed up in the club's steel vault,

115

surrounded by overturned tables, I was armed with a shotgun, a rifle, and a pistol. Nicknamed the Celebrity Room, my vault was lined with pictures of noted entertainers. It was a place where I took my guests to have a drink in private. From the vault, located halfway down the bar, I kept an eye on the front vestibule. If my dog barked, I was prepared to take out any intruders. That night the police often came by to check on me. One of the officers, a sergeant whom I had befriended, gave me a handful of bullets. He said, "Mr. Wilson I do not want anything to happen to you. I wish you would go home." I replied, "I have no home. The police tore it up." "But we can't stop the people from coming in here," warned the officer.

I said, "Tell the sons of bitches I'm in here—me, my dog and my shotgun. Send 'em on in." I explained to the officer that I had to stay in my place to protect it from being burned. I told him, "If I lose this place, I'll have to walk back to South Carolina." He then looked at me and gave me another handful of bullets.

That evening I was standing on the stoop of my club when two policemen told me, "Hey, boy, get off those steps." I defiantly retorted, "I'm not going anywhere. I own these steps." Later, I told Inspector Morgan about my treatment and he told these officers to apologize.

I also saw five members of the Navy Shore Patrol. Dressed in white uniforms, three of them carried rifles with fixed bayonets, their non-enlisted officer carried a .45 pistol, and the black shore patrolman, since the police and the military did want armed blacks patrolling the streets, only carried a billy club. If that black sailor had tried to arrest anyone on Hastings, the neighborhood residents would have torn him apart.

Most of the black policemen were called off the streets and made to stay at their station houses. Two black officers were my friends—Jesse Stewart and Willie Williams, a tough young man and a good fistfighter who had worked for me at the Forest Club. Officers Williams and Stewart were on duty during the riot, when a black undertaker near Theodore Street reported to police that these two officers failed to arrest some people they saw committing a crime. Officers Williams and Stewart were suspended and charged with neglect of duty.

116

Knowing the character of these officers, I did not believe the charge. It smacked of wrongdoing and conspiracy. Anyone familiar with Willie Williams knew he wouldn't run from death. I contacted Jap Sneed, owner of Club Three Sixes, and we went down to the station house and put up bond for them. Despite the gross misconduct and violent behavior of the white officers, I don't think any were charged. Yet these two black officers, based on the report of one individual, were immediately thrown in jail. In 1992, nearly fifty years after the riot, Mr. Stewart invited me to come down to the Detroit City County Building auditorium to a ceremony that presented Willie Williams and him with an official notice exonerating them from the charge. They received a plaque citing their bravery. Willie Williams never did learn about this. He had already passed away.

During the riot, I heard white policemen asking each other, "Did you get a rabbit today?" They came to treat blacks on the street as if they were animals, killing them as if it had become a sport. These Southern white policemen lived under the shadow of prejudice. They had been raised to look upon the black man as their servant. They failed to realize times had changed.

From witnesses in the neighborhood, I learned how William Hardges, one of my Golden Gloves boxers, had been killed by police. Unlike the official account published in the press, eyewitnesses recounted how Hardges's sister had been knocked down by a policeman. Seeing his sister knocked to the pavement, Hardges knocked down the officer. Witness to Hardges's "assault," another patrolman came up from behind and blew the young man's head off.

Despite the immoral actions of a number of patrolmen, I worked with Inspector Morgan to clear the streets of roaming crowds. Standing on top of a patrol car in the middle of Hastings, I shouted, "You cannot fight bullets with bricks! Please go on home to your families." Thankfully, many of these people turned around and went home. The police put up a blockade around the neighborhood which prevented residents from traveling outside the area. Since the stores were in shambles, I handed out food from the Forest Club's storeroom. To acquire milk for the infants and young folks, Inspector Morgan gave me permission to cross

117

the blockade. I made daily trips, returning with food and cigarettes.

Several weeks later, following the departure of federal troops who had occupied Paradise Valley, there continued to be an atmosphere of racial tension. During his rounds on Hastings Street, a racist policeman often came in the Forest Club, pushing and shoving customers. He walked in one night, harassed a black man and his white girlfriend, and then took them to jail. I warned him he had no right to intimidate my customers. "Listen, you can't do this in here. I control this place."

"What you gonna do about it?" asked the officer.

I replied, "I don't know what I'm going to do about it. What are you going to do about it?"

He told me, "I heard about you."

And I said, "Yes, and I heard about you and the way you treat people. I want to let you know I don't appreciate you, and I don't like the way you come in here and harass my customers."

He wrote me up for disorderly conduct, which led to my appearance before the Liquor Control Commission. After the riot many vindictive members of the police department blamed me for starting the race riot. Although I was one of the only black men who worked with the police and helped the community during the shooting, killing, and robbing, the authorities continued to blame me. When I appeared before the Liquor Control Commission, they questioned me about the guns that I kept in the bar, one of which was not registered because it had been given to me during the riot. With these charges, my liquor license was threatened. I hired Attorney Cecil Rowlette of the firm Rowlette and Lewis. At the meeting I asked Mr. Rowlette if I could question the officer. After obtaining approval from the board, Mr. Rowlette said there were no objections. I walked right in front of this officer, stared in his face, and asked him where he was from.

"From Alabama," he answered.

"Why don't you like colored folks?"

He didn't say a word.

"Why did you harass that colored man and his girlfriend?"

He was still silent.

"Your honor," I said, "This is the seed of hatred and discrimination, the very cause of the race riot. This man sitting there is a menace. He is full of malice against black people and should be fired. I know a great number of good policemen who abide by rules and regulations. This one is not one of them. I am going to file a complaint with the police commissioner to get him off the street because it is he and others like him who will cause another race riot." Without inhibition I walked all over this man. During my statement, the room remained deathly quiet. After my testimony, the board cleared me of the charges.

Later, I volunteered as a witness to report the harassing of residents by police. My defiant attitude did not go unnoticed. I upset the authorities and the police. I believed my actions were justified because the riot didn't have to happen. It emerged out of unchecked and innate hate. The police had been warned; they were well aware of the events on the street. Today the Urban League honors me for my role in helping people and black businessmen during the riot, especially speaking out against the brutality of the police. But back then few people worked with me to voice opposition.

As the events of the riot passed and Hastings returned to normal, black and white patrons filled the nightclubs of Paradise Valley. In 1948 G. Mennen Williams, heir to the multimillion-dollar Mennen company and Democratic candidate for governor, campaigned at the Forest Club. This was the first time in the history of Detroit politics that a white political candidate campaigned in front of black folks. He became the first politician to take a person-to-person approach in attracting the black vote. Mr. Williams was a fine gentleman, but, being a millionaire and a resident of Grosse Pointe, I don't believe he was comfortable around black people. He had never had much association with blacks. When he came to my place, he brought his wife Nancy and campaign managers Martha and Hicks Griffiths. The club was packed wall to wall with my black customers. I escorted Mr. Williams and his wife through the crowd and seated them at a booth. I encouraged him to meet people and shake hands. He did, and he had a good time, too.

119

In October 1949 I got involved with the appearance of Communist spokesman Paul Robeson. This was a month after white rioters attacked Robeson outside Peekskill, New York. Things were pretty hot for Robeson, but I didn't know anything about Peekskill.[9] When Robeson came to speak in Detroit, he was denied use of downtown theaters and lodgings at the Book Cadillac Hotel. Robeson's isolation from civic and mainstream political circles motivated his Detroit left-wing supporters to form the Detroit Committee to Welcome Robeson.[10] Under the leadership of Erma Henderson,[11] the committee sought a place for him to speak. When Robeson arrived in Detroit, I was up north at

---

9. On August 27, 1949, an angry mob, in protest of Robeson's appearance, attacked 200 concert-goers at the Lakeland Acres picnic grounds near Peekskill, New York. With the outbreak of violence the show was canceled. At a rescheduled appearance on September 4, at the Hollow Brook Golf Course three miles from Peekskill, Robeson performed in the midst of a 900-police vanguard. Despite police protection, 145 concert-goers were injured by an anti-Robeson mob. Transported by a car convoy, Robeson and his supporters met a hail of rocks and projectiles. To protect Robeson and the other passengers, blankets were placed in car windows. While Robeson lay on the floor of his departing automobile, two trade union bodyguards covered the singer with their bodies.

Traditionally supported by Detroit's labor force and political leaders, Robeson, during his visit to Detroit, found himself alienated from industrial union support and city hall. Amid the anti-communist crusade of the cold war, he was not allowed to rent downtown Detroit concert halls and was refused accommodations at the world-famous Book Cadillac Hotel.

10. In the *Detroit News* the Detroit police department reported that the Detroit Committee to Welcome Robeson was a "secret committee" of the Michigan Civil Rights Congress—a committee that was "on the United States Attorney General's list of subversive organizations."

11. According to Erma Henderson, "Since the Peekskill outrage, many people have joined our committee and have lauded Robeson's courageous stand." "Paul Robeson Scheduled to Sing and Speak Here," *Detroit Tribune*, September 24, 1949, p. 7.

Idlewild, but later, back in town, I was having lunch at the Gotham Hotel when a group of people approached my table. Erma Henderson introduced me to the head of the group—a man who explained that his organization wanted to use the Forest Club for Robeson's appearance.

Though I had met Robeson in New York, I had reservations about his relations with black people. Robeson seemed all right in the early days, but after he stopped coming around to the black neighborhoods, I grew disappointed with him. I bluntly told the man, "I don't believe Mr. Robeson has any interest in coming to speak to my black folks on Hastings Street." "No, no, no," he interrupted. "Mr. Robeson told me he wants to speak at your club and sent me personally to talk to you." "Why?" I asked, questioning his intentions. "Mr. Robeson usually speaks at the Lafayette Theater." The man responded, "But they won't let him speak downtown." He informed me that discrimination prevented Robeson from appearing downtown. Since I was always willing to fight against segregation, I decided to support the group's cause. As a businessman I was honored to have a big name like Paul Robeson appear at my club. I told the man, "I don't mind if Mr. Robeson wants to speak at my place, but on one condition—that he makes the price low enough for the black folks on Hastings Street to attend the appearance."

I rented my place, just as I had to the auto unions, to any organization that offered to help the black community of Detroit. I believe a person should be free to voice his opinions. I have been a member of the Urban League since the early 1940s. Despite my opposition to some of the league's policies, I still make donations because of the economic foundation they provide. I am also a member of the NAACP, although I have only attended about two meetings in my life. I don't agree with most of its theories, but I support its efforts to help our people.

When I agreed to host the concert, however, I didn't know about the Peekskill riot. I was unaware that Robeson's appearance would set off such a harsh reaction from city hall and the police. The next day, after my meeting with Robeson's group, Detroit Police Commissioner Harry S. Toy told the citizens not to worry because they were going to surround the club with a special vanguard of policemen, made up of mounted officers, patrol cars, riot squads, police commandos, and special details armed with tear gas. Commissioner Toy made a public statement vindictively claiming that Sunnie Wilson started the 1943 race riot. One local black newspaper ran an article alerting readers that Robeson was to appear at the Forest Club—the place "where the 1943 Detroit riot began." Veterans groups like Amvets, American Legion, and the Catholic War Veterans stated they were going to boycott Robeson's appearance.[12]

As public criticism mounted, I grew nervous. Police Inspector William Bert came to the Forest Club and told me that Commissioner Toy wanted me to come down and speak to him. Because of his comments condemning me for the race riot, I wasn't about to go to the commissioner's office; I wanted him to come to me. I told Inspector Bert that I opposed Commissioner Toy's plans to place the police on my roof and around my building. As the owner I had my own security men and bouncers and I didn't need the police intimidating my patrons with an open display of weapons.

At the Mark Twain, where I was living, I began to get threatening phone calls. "You black son of a bitch, we're gonna drop a bomb on that damn hotel. Watch your step. Every time you walk out the door, we will be waiting for you!" Though I had never carried a gun in my life, I now packed a gold-plated pistol. Every time I left the hotel, I took two bodyguards with me. Instead of sleeping in my room near the street, I moved to a room in the back of the hotel.

One night I looked out the window and noticed a crowd gathering on the lawn in front of the hotel. I thought the crowd was coming to lynch me. By the time I went outside, about five hundred people stood on my lawn. To my relief the crowd turned out to be some Wayne University students, members of a Com-

---

12. "Legion Plans to Ignore Paul Robeson Concert," *Michigan Chronicle,* October 1, 1949, p. 7. In the *Detroit News,* members of the AMVETS, the American Legion, and the Catholic War Veterans warned Detroiters to "keep out of the vicinity of the Forest Club, 700 avenue east, where [Robeson] is scheduled to sing and talk [at] 7:00 p.m."

munist group, who told me: "You're a man with American dreams, and we stand by you." This crowd shouted, "We're with you!" I knew the crowd was large, because the next day I looked out and saw that my grass had been trampled flat against the ground. I was also supported by the Fur and Leather Workers' union. They gave me their number to contact them in case I ran into trouble.

Despite the support given to me by the union and Wayne State students, the threats to my life forced me to consider canceling Robeson's Forest Club appearance. But I also reasoned that since I was the owner of a license that guaranteed the right of public assembly, city hall had no legal right to tell me who could and couldn't appear at my place. I then sought the advice of Dr. Bennett and labor and civil rights activist Reverend Horace White, the pastor of the Plymouth Congregational Church. I had known Reverend White for some time and was aware of his expertise in public affairs. Reverend White was a brilliant thinker and speaker who earned his doctorate from Oberlin's School of Divinity. An experienced labor organizer and member of the Detroit Housing Commission, Reverend White had been an important figure during the 1939 Dodge Main and 1941 Ford strikes, as well as the 1942 Sojourner Truth housing incident. Together we devised a plan. To deceive city hall, we decided to announce the cancellation of the concert at my place.

At a meeting at the Mark Twain, I informed the group that I was going to cancel the concert. Erma Henderson and several of her committee people told me, with tears in their eyes, not to cancel. I explained to them and the other members that what had started out as a gesture of goodwill had turned ugly and that Robeson's appearance could cause a riot. On October 1, a week before the actual concert, the front page of the *Detroit Tribune* announced, "Paul Robeson Refused Use of the Forest Club Ballroom."

When word got out about my canceling the concert, Commissioner Toy called and invited me to meet with him. I agreed. Commissioner Toy held a meeting in his office. I called the newspaper reporters to be at the meeting. Accompanied by my lawyer, I entered Commissioner Toy's office and informed him that the reporters were outside in the hall. I told Commissioner Toy that our meeting was open to the press. With his approval, I opened the door and invited the reporters inside. I told the crowd, "My name is Sunnie Wilson, and I am an American citizen. I am not affiliated with any anti-American organization. I have a license so that anyone can rent my hall, same as the Lafayette and Masonic Halls."

Edwin Morgan, who had by that time been promoted to police superintendent, spoke up for me. "I have known Sunnie Wilson for twenty-five years," he said, "and I assure you he is not and has never been a Communist." I then told Commissioner Toy, "You don't have to worry about Sunnie Wilson anymore. I'm not hosting any concert. But I do hear that since Robeson can't speak at my place, he is going to move the gathering downtown to Grand Circus Park." The last thing in the world the city wanted was a second Peekskill riot in the heart of Detroit. With my announcement, city hall decided to support Robeson's appearance at the Forest Club.[13]

The night before the concert, the fire department came in and demanded that, in order to comply with code, each row of folding chairs be wired together. Volunteers stayed up all night wiring each chair leg to leg. Early the next evening, Sunday, October 9, one thousand policemen, under the command of Superintendent Morgan, surrounded the building. Across the street in the crowd of observers, I saw Mayor Eugene Van Antwerp and his people watching my place. I also saw Reverend Horace White. Like Mayor Antwerp, Horace White showed up to help deter any trouble. I believe the mayor and Reverend White both feared the police department and its willingness to use violence. For it was the police who fueled the fire of the '43 riot.

---

13. The night before the concert the *Michigan Chronicle* (October 8, 1949, p. 22) observed: "Quite a mess has developed in regard to the use of the Forest Club by Paul Robeson. . . . Rumor has it tremendous pressure has been put on Sonny [*sic*] Wilson, owner of the club, to break his contract with the Committee to Welcome Robeson. Sonny [*sic*] in the meantime doesn't know just what to do because of the question of his liquor license."

To incite the crowd outside Communist agitators placed microphones in the hall. These outside agitators were revolutionary Communists and their goal was overthrow the status quo. We found microphone cords that ran outside the building and pulled them out. Whoever these people were, they did not belong to Robeson's group. Robeson was there to sing and speak, not cause a riot.

Coleman Young was in charge of the committee's security. He and David Moore, along with another man, Chris Bellinson, escorted Robeson into the club. Coleman and the other bodyguards wore steel helmets. Outside, lines of people wrapped around the building. Long, black limousines, filled with Wayne State professors and wealthy Grosse Pointe residents, lined Hastings Street. Eighteen hundred listeners crowded my hall and several hundred more could not gain admittance. There were more white people at the event than black folks. Everything went smoothly—no violence, no shooting, just long lines of Communist supporters. It turned out to be a white party rather than a black party. In many ways having Paul Robeson speak at my place, in the midst of the cold war, was like inviting the kiss of death. I remain thankful to Reverend Horace White and Dr. Robert Bennett, who stood behind me in a time of crisis.

Down at city hall they didn't forget my efforts to bring Robeson to my club. For months afterward, building inspectors came knocking at my door. One by one they came, demanding that I move doorways, reroute plumbing, and install new heating. I had no choice but to comply with these codes, and they cost me a large amount of money in repairs and remodeling.

But I didn't let the events following Robeson's appearance interfere with my roster of entertainment. In 1949 I brought in the bands of Charlie Ventura and Woody Herman, whose big band featured my friend saxophonist Gene "Red Top" Ammons, bassist Oscar Pettiford and drummer Shadow Wilson. To give the evening a promotional touch of class, I blocked off Hastings and set up searchlights. Herman was so impressed he told me, "Sunnie Wilson, goddamn it! This is Hollywood!"

Around this time I also brought the great doo-wop singing group the Ravens, who topped the charts in 1947 with their rendition of "Old Man River." I brought them in from New York, along with their back-up band, for a show at the Forest Club. They appeared on a Friday night, but a heavy rain made the turn-out very slim. Since I didn't have anything booked for the next night, I invited them to do a Saturday performance. They agreed.

I then contacted my disc-jockey friend Leroy White at WJLB, and he put in a plug for the show. He plugged for me like he did for black politicians or anybody else. Leroy was the most popular disc jockey in town, an irascible scrapper who loved to confront people. On the air he would always say: "Tell 'em Leroy sent you." When the Jewish merchants on Hastings Street didn't like a customer, they would send him to a bad place with the recommendation, "Tell 'em Leroy sent you." One night at the Forest Club an overflow crowd of young people stood outside the door and shouted, "Leroy sent us!" I told them, "You'd better go get him then, because you're not getting in here until I have the room for you." Not long after, I put a sign on the front window that read, "Leroy Just Left." With Leroy's advertising, the second show was a big success. The Ravens and I split the profits and in doing so, I was able to cover my losses from the Friday performance.

Besides big bands, I had local pianists play for my customers in the lounge. A local character, pianist and singer Detroit Count, came in my place about every night. His 1948 piano-rap hit "Hastings Street Opera" talked about me and all the people along the avenue. The idea to record the song came from two white men, two street hustlers. They put up the money and bought the Count a tuxedo, a hat, and some shoes. Though Joe Von Battle recorded the song in his studio on Hastings and leased it to King Records, these two fellas sold the discs on corners up and down the street. It became a local hit.

Unfortunately, the Count never took care of himself. He drank quite heavily. The Count came from Tennessee. My friend Roy Lightfoot first heard him and gave him a job at his B & C Club. As long as I knew the Count, I never knew him to hold a steady job. He supported himself by sitting in and playing at all the Valley bars—Roy Lightfoot's or the Frolic—wherever he could rustle up some money. If a club had a piano, you could bet the Count would soon be there playing on it. People requested his hit "Hastings Street Opera," a tune that he could stretch out for a hour. A lot of the time, listeners would ask him to stop playing it, because they wanted to hear something else. He came into my place weekly. Unfortunately, by the time he got to my place, he was usually half plastered.

When the Count was sober, though, he was no slouch on the keyboard. The Count could play the blues. Sitting down at my piano, he would play a few numbers and then ask me for five dollars. If I didn't give him five dollars, he got mad. Sometimes I slipped him some money for food. The Count worked just enough to get along. Back then you could get an inexpensive hotel room for a few dollars a night. Everybody loved the Count. Whenever he got into trouble he would look to me for protection. If anybody bothered him, he'd say, "You better leave me alone, or Sunnie Wilson will come after you."

With all this going on, I decided to make some changes of my own. I updated my entertainment at the club. To entertain the crowds at the Forest Club's 1950 New Year's Eve party, I brought in the band of saxophonist Illinois Jacquet and singer Madeline Greene, a former singer with the Earl Hines band. A few months later, I opened my revamped show bar and hired my good friend from Chicago, Joe "Ziggy" Johnson. Several months earlier, Ziggy moved from Chicago's Beige Room to the Club Valley, formerly the Three Sixes, on Adams. After awhile he wasn't doing well financially, so I invited him to work at my place as a show manager. I brought him into the Forest Club and gave him a room, Ziggy's Blue Room.[14]

Ziggy grew up in Chicago where he studied dance under Paul Ash. He was a good basketball player and athlete, but his first love was show business. He danced from Chicago to Atlantic City, all over the country, and had worked as producer and dancer

---

14. An article in the *Michigan Chronicle* characterized Wilson's new "Theater Show Bar" in the Forest Club and Joe "Ziggy's Blue Room" as "an atmospherish little nook that is growing in popularity at the Wilson Show Bar." "Line-up New Starline Friday at Sunnie Wilson's," *Michigan Chronicle*, June 10, 1950, p. 21.

at Joe Louis's and Charlie Glenn's short-lived Rhumboogie Club in Chicago.[15] Count Basie, who worked with Ziggy in Atlantic City, told how my friend was "right up there in the same class with Larry Steele when it came to putting together great shows with beautiful chorus girls, singers, and comedians. When it came to big production numbers with fabulous costumes, he was the greatest."

Ziggy had an affinity for straw hats and could flip them and twirl them with precision. His favorite song was Duke Ellington's "Satin Doll," a song that lent itself to the choreography of pretty chorus and show girls.

Joe Ziggy and I always had a good-time competition going between us, like the time when bandleader Lucius "Lucky" Millinder stayed at the Mark Twain. Apart from being a orchestra leader, Millinder worked for the *Pittsburgh Courier* and was a disc jockey and fortune teller. Like Cab Calloway, Millinder didn't play or write music; he was strictly a bandleader. While at the Mark Twain, he bought Joe Ziggy and me each a suit. He gave me a sweater, too. Because Joe Ziggy didn't get a sweater, he got jealous and fell out with Lucky Millinder. I said, "Ziggy, what are you so mad about? You can't have everything."

After Ziggy debuted his revue show at the Forest Club in June 1951, he and I worked together for the senatorial elections of Charles Diggs Jr. and disc jockey Bristoe Bryant. Taking up the political torch from his father, Senator Charles Diggs Sr., Charles Jr. won the primary by a vote of 7,800 to 3,200. Using the Mark Twain as Diggs's campaign headquarters, Ziggy and I held rallies and broadcast live from the hotel. Our efforts helped Diggs win a senate seat in the Third District.

As the Mark Twain became a center for political activity, the

---

15. Joe Louis and Charlie Glenn, a sportsman and Cadillac salesman, purchased the club at 343 East Garfield in 1940, changing its name to the Rhumboogie Club. With Louis as the principal financial backer, Glenn hoped to build a nightclub to rival New York's Cotton Club and Chicago's Grand Terrace. Due to the back debt of ten thousand dollars in unpaid taxes, the Internal Revenue Service closed and padlocked the club's doors in 1947.

Forest Club hosted a number of different events. In 1951, I sponsored the *Michigan Chronicle* Home Service Exposition at the Forest Club. During the several days of the event, over twenty thousand people visited thirty booths occupied by black-owned businesses and organizations such as the NAACP College Fund, the Housewives League, Bay Furniture, the Great Lakes Mutual Life, Lester Brothers Coffee, and even Joe Louis Punch. To help publicize the exposition, Leroy White broadcast his show live from the stage of my club. The exhibitors sponsored a contest awarding three thousand dollars in prizes: gas ranges, refrigerators, tables, lamps, and the like.

At the end of 1951, however, my ten-year lease ran out at the Forest Club. To renew the lease, I had to bid for it. Two black investors approached me to buy the club. They had several white investors backing them, two of whom were lawyers. These people were damn near gangsters. They attempted to create pressure to take my license. News of their dealings got around to Morris Wasserman, and he held a meeting for me at the Flame Show Bar. To help me deal with these people, the Italian don sent his brother to the meeting. The investors came to the Flame. Frank warned them that his brother would be very upset if they didn't give me a good deal. One of the black investors introduced himself and said, "I don't want any trouble. I like all you boys."

Perturbed at this man's cocky attitude, I asked, "What's my name?" "Sunnie Wilson," he answered. "My name is not Sunnie Wilson, it is Mr. Wilson. Don't you ever forget it!" I looked around at this black man and then, pointing at his partners, said, "There are your 'boys.' Be careful, or we will kick all your asses." But without the money to challenge my adversaries, I was forced to sell my investment. I didn't like their aggressive attitude. To throw off their plans, I offered them the sale of my liquor license for the exorbitant sum of one hundred thousand dollars. Of course, they didn't agree, and bought the club without it.

In the midst of my trouble, my friends did not forget me. I asked them to each send me a dollar and I received a bushel basket full. They were there for me. During the last days of my ownership, the nightclub owners and businessmen of the Valley—Jap Sneed, drugstore magnate Sidney Barthwell and others—threw me a week-long party at my place, celebrating the club that, as the *Michigan Chronicle* stated, "brought history to the corner of Forest and Hastings."

The last night of the three-day event, at two o'clock in the morning, I took the stage and looking out at the audience, declared, "THIS IS IT!" I went on reminiscing about my days on the strip. Some say there were few in the house who didn't have tears in their eyes.[16]

The support shown to me by my fellow businessmen, however, did not diminish my anger over the harassment by the club's new buyers. I refused to leave completely on their terms. Before I moved out, I took out ten gallons of acid and poured it on my bowling alley. Then I took an axe and chopped up my bar. Everything I destroyed was mine. These investors never did get a liquor license, and they lost a lot of money. I walked out a free man in mind. What I did was wrong as a businessman. Yet no one could have me stopped at the time.

---

16. Bill Lane describes Wilson's closing celebration: "Sunnie Wilson, the little showman who lives up to every letter of his popular moniker, bowed out as pilot of goings-on around the corner of Forest and Hastings last Wednesday night." Bill Lane, "Swinging Down the Lane," *Michigan Chronicle,* February 3, 1951, p. 21.

◆ 6 ◆
Idlewild

L ocated in Lake County sixty-nine miles north of Grand
Rapids, Idlewild emerged between the 1920s and the 1950s
as the largest black resort in America, accommodating
many of the country's most distinguished African American families. Occupying thirty-six square miles, Idlewild was incorporated as
a section of Yates Township. Down through the years Idlewild has
been known as the Black Eden, Apollo of the North, and the Black
Las Vegas. In a period when blacks were denied access to white hotels
and vacation spots, Idlewild drew thousands of vacationers from
Ohio, Indiana, Illinois, and Missouri.

At the height of its popularity, Idlewild attracted weekend
crowds of over twenty thousand visitors, who came to fish, hunt, ride
horseback, and swim in the waters of Idlewild Lake. When crowds
filled hotels, visitors slept in cars or got permission to camp in cottage-
owners' backyards.

In the fall of 1915, after developing two other northern Michigan resorts, white real-estate investors—Erastus G. Branch and
Adelbert Branch—purchased a strip of land around Idlewild Lake.[1]

---

1. The Branch family migrated from Van Buren County in 1884
and arrived in Newago County around 1914. With the decline of the

Incorporated as the Idlewild Resort Corporation (IRC), the group purchased 2,700 acres of cut-over timberland. Parceling the land into 19,000 small plots, the IRC sold each 25-by-100-foot lot for thirty-five dollars: six dollars down and one dollar a week. To attract potential black investors the Branches changed the lake's name and the surrounding property to Idlewild.

The Branches contacted black Chicago real-estate salespeople— Wilbur Lemon, Mamye Lemon, Alvin E. Wright, and Madolin Wright—who launched a Midwestern publicity campaign, advertising the purchase of Idlewild real estate on billboards and street-cars, and sponsored free train excursions to the island.

Among the first notable African Americans to purchase land at Idlewild was Dr. Daniel Hale Williams, who in 1893 became the first surgeon to enter successfully the chest cavity and suture the heart of a living patient. Following the 1917 acquisition of a large tract of land, Williams built a subdivision and sold property to such famous African Americans as civil-rights activist and co-founder of the NAACP W. E. B. Du Bois, cosmetic giant Madame C. J. Walker, and Cleveland-born novelist Charles Waddell Chesnutt. After learning about the resort from his wife Susan, Chesnutt and his family spent several summers in a rented cottage at Idlewild. Eventually Chesnutt built a cottage, which he continued to visit until his death in 1932.

Originally Idlewild Island was connected to the mainland by wood-plank footbridges. In 1917 Erastus Branch constructed a log "auto bridge" to accommodate the increasing number of lot owners and vacationers. On surrounding lots Branch constructed 10-by-12-foot wooden platforms over which tents were pitched. Eventually the canvas tents were replaced by wood-plank bungalows, known by Idlewilders as doghouses. These one-door cottages usually contained two cots, a crude nightstand, and a pitcher and bowl.

In 1921 The IRC turned the resort over to the Idlewild Lot Owners Association and within several years the association was able to attract numerous investors to the northern resort commu-

lumber trade and its recreational activities, the Branches were the first real-estate investors in the area to recognize the potential of a local tourist trade.

nity. That same year Du Bois informed his readers, in the NAACP's magazine The Crisis, *of the IRC's fair practices. "Now white men developed Idlewild," wrote Du Bois. "They have made money on the operation. . . . But they have not been hogs. Idlewild is worth every penny."*[2]

In the early 1920s a clubhouse was built for family gatherings and nighttime entertainment. In a 1923 letter written to a friend, Chesnutt wrote of his attraction to the island's clubhouse: "Last summer I spent my vacation at a summer resort, and every night I would go up to the Clubhouse where there was a good band and dancing floor, and dance the whole program through to the Home Waltz."[3] *That same year, on October 26, 1923, Susie S. Bantom became Idlewild's first postmaster.*

Over the next decades Idlewild grew into a thriving black community, boasting a post office and fire department, as well as several hotels and retail stores. Throughout the 1930s, The Crisis *advertised Idlewild resort accommodations, such as Virgil Williams's Oakmere Hotel, where Detroiter Sunnie Wilson rented a year-round room. In the woods of this idyllic northern resort Wilson found not only a relaxing atmosphere and exciting nightly entertainment, but a sense of community with African Americans from throughout the country. Active in political and social developments in Idlewild, Wilson became president of the Detroit Idlewilders in 1952. That same year a* Michigan Chronicle *columnist named Wilson one of Idlewild's "most honorary citizens" and "eloquent boosters."*[4] *Noting Wilson's popularity at the resort, Joe "Ziggy" Johnson wrote, "You'd think Sunnie Wilson was mayor here, as he seems to be loved by all."*[5]

---

2. Quoted in Ric Bohy, "Paradise Laid to Rest: Nightclubs Are Gone, but Idlewild Thrives," *Detroit News,* August 19, 1985, sec. A, p. 9.

3. Quoted in Francis Keller, *An American Crusade: The Life of Charles Waddell Chesnutt* (Provo, Utah: Brigham Young University Press, 1978), 267.

4. Frank M. Seymour, "See More with Seymour," *Michigan Chronicle,* June 21, 1952, p. 21.

5. Ziggy Johnson, "Zaggin' with Ziggy," *Michigan Chronicle,* May 31, 1952, p. 19.

Nineteen fifty-one was a busy year. After I sold the Forest Club, I bought a small hotel on West Grand Boulevard and Grand River, the Sunnie Wilson Hotel. Not far from my hotel on the west side, Edmoor Bertrand owned the Crystal Show Bar on Grand River. He booked a lot of top-name entertainment, such as the great tenor saxophonist Lester "The Prez" Young and Julian "Cannonball" Adderly. Most of the musicians and entertainers who played the west side of town stayed at the Mark Twain or the Sunnie Wilson Hotel. The Prez always wore his big porkpie hat. He kept to himself and didn't say much to anyone. After he checked in, he would lock himself in his room. He only came out when it was time to go to a gig. When Miles Davis played at the Blue Bird Inn on Tireman and Beechwood, he often stayed at the Sunnie Wilson Hotel. Broke and without a car, he would walk eight blocks to his job at the Blue Bird.

One year later, I became president and founding member of the Detroit Idlewilders Club, an organization dedicated to investors, property owners, and vacationers of the country's oldest and most popular black resort.[6] We founded the Idlewild Club in the home of Mr. and Mrs. Joseph Branam at 300 Arden Park. The Branams were the successful owners of the Golden Dairy Milk company. Among the guests and founding members were Attorney Joseph A. Craigen, newspaper writer Isola Graham, businessman Clarence Brown, and Lucille Watts. Together we nominated the officers of the club. I was elected president, Craigen vice president, and Joseph Branam treasurer. Our founding motto stated our mutual pledge to aid and support charitable and civic endeavors and to promote social entertaining and recreation. We gathered at various members' homes until increasing membership prompted us to gather at the Mark Twain and Garfield Hotels.

---

6. Prominent Detroit Idlewilders included Charles Diggs, John Hill Matlocks, Robert Bennett, J. J. McClendon, Andrew Jackson, Joseph and Sulee Stinson, Joe "Ziggy" Johnson, Randolph Wallace, Judge C. W. Jones, Phil Giles, Callie Walker, and Hobart Taylor, and Maxine Powell. "Bits and Pieces," *Michigan Chronicle*, March 4, 1989, sec. C, p. 4.

Some forty years prior to our establishing the Idlewilders
Club, the Branch brothers founded the northern resort. Discrimination created Idlewild, practices that sought to prohibit blacks
from access to our nation's resorts. Idlewild was created out of
blacks' need to find a resort area unspoiled by racism, where they
would be free from intimidation and violence. It was this sense of
freedom that drew wealthy blacks from their New York estates
and Midwestern homes to the woods and beautiful lakes around
Idlewild.

During the 1930s Michigan had several small black
resorts—one at Brighton and another near Fenton. During World
War II, I owned a farm off the highway not far from Fenton.
Property didn't sell much at that time. It was a nice place, but
nothing special. It had a small, stagnant muck lake. I kept two
dogs there. Purchasing it for seven thousand dollars, I bought the
farm for its two thousand chickens, which I sold for two dollars
each. I eventually gave the land to my employees.

Whenever I got the chance, I often visited spots in northern
Michigan. I remember visiting a friend, Mr. Austin, a black St.
Louis cab-company owner, who had a place called the Octagon
Castle. I met him at the Forest Club and he invited me up north
to his place. Located back in the woods, the Octagon Castle was,
according to local history, originally owned by wealthy Germans.
They used a large box radio to communicate with their homeland
during the war. It was a very strange place. The main room had a
bear rug on the floor and bunk beds, each inscribed with a different month of the year. There was a mess hall and servants'
quarters. Mr. Austin invited me to stay the night, but I felt uneasy
over the strange atmosphere and politely declined.

Though I had been to several places in northern Michigan,
Idlewild eventually became my regular destination. When I first
went to Idlewild, I knew nothing about it. I drove my girlfriend,
her son, and her mother up there in the 1930s. Arriving at night,
I took a room at a boarding house. I soon discovered, however,
that the homes didn't have indoor plumbing or electric lights.
You had to use flashlights. I thought it was the worst place in the
world. But when I awoke the next morning at sunrise and saw the

beauty that surrounded me, I fell in love with the place. I suddenly realized its great potential.

During its first years, from 1915 to 1916, the island had only small one-bed houses and had yet to see commercial development. The island was originally owned by the famous Chicago surgeon Dr. Daniel H. Williams. In 1920 Dr. Williams built a small cottage and named it Oakmere. Across the street from his residence, he built a small park with gravel walks and a summer pavilion. He, too, opened a two-story hotel which, like his home and neighboring park, he named Oakmere.

When he died in 1931, Dr. Williams willed the island to his sister Virgil Williams. Virgil Williams was a very light-complected woman who was born in France. After her brother's death, she came from her home in England to look after the island. Back in America, she married Mr. Williams, the owner of a Chicago theater, who had been married to Mr. Roxborough's ex-wife, Cutie. As owner of the Oakmere, Mrs. Williams ran a respectable hotel. She did not allow unmarried couples to stay on the island and if she found them out, they were asked to leave. I rented a year-round room at the Oakmere. In my room I kept whiskey for my guests, but I wouldn't let them touch my champagne.

As time passed and the Williamses grew older, they put the island up for sale. They wanted to give me the island, but I turned down the offer. I helped them divide the land up into lots. I located two surveyors and negotiated the island's sale price of sixty thousand dollars. Grateful for my assistance, the Williamses wanted to reward me. I refused money, but told them I was interested in an old dog that lived on the island named Mama. They sold the island and I got that old dog.

Another Chicago family responsible for the flowering of Idlewild were the Wilsons. In the 1920s Herman and Lela G. Wilson purchased property around Idlewild. A short, dignified woman, Lela Wilson was born in Tennessee and moved to Illinois with her parents. Later she became a real-estate saleswoman for Mr. Erastus Branch. When the Wilsons sold a lot, they reinvested the money in land around Idlewild. The Wilsons bought the Frank Haven Farm near Paradise Lake. In the early days, this section was known as Paradise Patch, in reference to what Southerners called a Negro patch, a small black-owned parcel of land. The Wilsons, however, expanded their investment and developed this area into a subdivision, naming it Paradise Gardens. This section is still platted on the township map as Paradise.

Following land development by the Williams and the Wilsons, the next important boon for the area came with the introduction of electricity. It brought Idlewild great prosperity. Electrical contractor Henry A. Gregory installed a Delmore generator system, which resulted in the construction of large summer homes and hotels. Around this time, the Wilsons built a very beautiful two-story, stone home. The locals say Lela had those stones hauled from the lake day and night, until there were enough to build her place. In the early years the Wilsons ran a store out of their garage and later opened a grocery store across the street. Lela Wilson and I were so close that people thought she was my aunt. When she died, they paid me respect as if she was one of my family.

During the 1930s and 1940s, Idlewild remained a place for well-to-do black cottage owners and vacationers. About sixteen miles from Idlewild, the black resort of Woodland emerged as an exclusive spot for wealthy blacks, and had one of the prettiest lakes in the country. It was originally established as a retirement spot. Visitors rented cottages, meals included. If the residents wanted to make a little noise and take in some music, they went over to Idlewild.

When I first went to Idlewild, it was still a dry section. The Williamses opened the Purple Palace, the first nightspot on the island. Located across from the Oakmere Hotel, the club was a bring-your-own spot that featured small bands. They were nothing fancy or big name, just nice little groups to keep you dancing and having a good time.

At the same time that the Williamses had the Purple Palace, the El Morocco existed as the only dining establishment. A one-story wooden building located back in the woods on Nelson Road, the El Morocco served fine food. For years it remained a breakfast and after-hours spot, a place where you brought your own set up—whiskey, champagne, and the like. The Morocco's owner, Raja, was a tall, thin black man who wore a turban. A man of few words, Raja rarely spoke to his customers. He married a white woman, a lumber baron's daughter. To keep the customers entertained during the late-night hours, the El Morocco featured musical entertainment.

Around this time, Chicago's Jones Boys, George and Mac, bought homes in Idlewild, and Ed bought his mother a home. Mac had a party every year. He'd charge admission and have a live band. When his wife died, George Jones closed up the cottage he had built for her at Idlewild. It had a separate garage and servants' quarters. George hired a guard to watch the place during the summers. When they opened the house a few years ago, everything was on the dresser just like it had been before she died.

One time when Joe Louis and I were on a trip with the Brown Bombers softball team in Grand Rapids, we decided to go up to Idlewild. I had to convince Joe to go up to Idlewild because he had never been there. He didn't think anything worth seeing was up there. But at my insistence, he decided to go with me. When we got to Idlewild, we broke into one of the Joneses' houses. We took their speedboat out on the lake. Afterward, we left them a note thanking them for the use of their place. After that, Joe and I often vacationed at Idlewild. Joe met some interesting people and he liked the pretty girls.

During the late 1940s, I traveled to Idlewild regularly. Whenever I could get away, I would get in my Pontiac convertible, take the top down, and drive with the gas pedal to the floor until I reached the north woods. I stayed at the Williams's Oakmere Hotel next to the Flamingo Club. Back then, Idlewild was filled with small rooming houses. Eventually, Phil Giles bought the Oakmere in 1949 and renamed it the Phil Giles Hotel.

By the early 1950s, the legalization of liquor drew even more celebrities and vacationers to Idlewild. Mr. William Green, Callie Walker, and I canvassed the community and got the legalization of liquor passed. We contacted Governor Mennen Williams to come and visit the resort. This part of Lake County was a Republican stronghold before the 1940s. We wanted to stop the flow of money from the pocketbooks of black folks who had to purchase liquor in nearby Baldwin, just a few miles west of Idlewild. Originally the seat of Lake County was in Chase and later was moved to Baldwin in 1875. Baldwin was an old lumbertown that attracted hundreds of Swedes, Finns, and Scots who came to move the cut timber south on the Muskegon River. At its peak, Baldwin had twenty-six bars.

Although it was a nice, small town, Baldwin upheld segregation in several places of business. Together with Attorney Oscar Baker of Bay City, I fought to abolish discrimination in Baldwin. When the store owners thought we were going to picket their establishments, they agreed without protest to end their discriminatory practices. The owner of the town's theater was especially cooperative and invited blacks to enter all the sections of his movie house.

After that, my main concern was attaining the legalization of liquor in Idlewild.[7] Receiving our invitation, Governor Williams informed us that he couldn't make the date and sent his wife, Nancy, instead. Walking through Idlewild, she never saw so many black folks in her life. After liquor came in, an imaginary line was drawn between Paradise and Idlewild, designating Paradise as the place where you could raise hell and Idlewild as a quieter, family-oriented community. Paradise was quiet until they brought whiskey in.

During the campaign to bring liquor to the island, a retired lawyer won the office of county prosecutor, marking the first time a black man had been elected to this position in Lake County. But unknown to my associates and me, this man turned out to be a hawk. He conducted raids on after-hours places in Idlewild and Paradise and put many people in jail.

Following the legalization of liquor, however, Idlewild became even more popular. With the legalization of liquor, along with the winning of vacation time by the United Auto Workers union, working-class customers came streaming in from Saginaw, Grand Rapids, and other outlying areas. To handle the crowds there were several good-sized hotels. The Casa Blanca was built in 1949 by W. C. M. Coombs, a Detroit architect and builder of West Indian descent. It was a nice, two-story, stucco-and-wood

---

7. Mr. Wilson is uncertain of the date here, but believes this took place between 1949 and 1951.

139

establishment. Margret Walker owned the Rainbow Manor. On the south side of Idlewild was a house of prostitution, the Eagle's Nest. An establishment made up of a string of small buildings, the Eagle's Nest had a real stuffed eagle at its entrance.

Along with these establishments existed an array of top entertainment. The area's first premier nightspot, the Paradise housed the 220-seat Fiesta Room, which booked big-scale productions. Over the years it remained the hot spot of the Paradise section. Booking at the club was handled by Saginaw businessman Arthur Braggs, a big fella whom musicians and customers called Big Daddy. The Paradise Club was located on Paradise Lake next to Wilson's grocery store. The Fiesta Room brought in national stars and acts, such as comedian George Kirby, Della Reese, Jackie Wilson, T-Bone Walker, Al Hibbler, Bill Doggett, Sarah Vaughan, Dinah Washington, Peg Leg Bates, and the up-and-coming Motown act, the Four Tops. These entertainers drew so many people that those who couldn't get in for the first performance waited outside for the second show.

Out of the Fiesta Room, Braggs managed the Idlewild Revue produced by Joe Ziggy. The show had chorus girls and beautiful show girls who walked the stage. Braggs took the annual revue on the road. Over the years, the show billed such names as T-Bone Walker, singer Lavern Baker, and the Four Tops. The revue played houses around the country, including Detroit's Flame Show Bar. In the early sixties the revue brought in exotic dancers all the way from Mexico.

The second nightclub to open was the Flamingo. After purchasing a plot of land from the Wilsons on Idlewild, Phil Giles and his wife Bea, owners of Detroit's Hotel Giles on Piquette, opened the Flamingo Club. Behind the Flamingo's white-painted, cement-block exterior was a bar room and main entertainment room with an elevated stage. The main entertainment room had a long, wooden bar. On the walls were hand-painted murals of tropical scenery. Although many of the shows at the Flamingo had chorus girls, they were small productions—good, but not anything you would see in Las Vegas or Atlantic City. Most of the groups came out of Detroit and Grand Rapids, primarily small groups and combos with musicians like saxophonist

Choker Campbell, who was the leader of the Flamingo's house band. One of the many vocalists to appear at the club was "Detroit's Queen of the Blues," Alberta Adams. Singers and entertainers at the club worked three shows a day. Phil Giles also featured an amateur show hosted by all the clubs. Sometimes I would serve as emcee. The show later moved to the Lot Owners' Association.

Once the cabarets started having music and whiskey, the white people came to Idlewild. Sometimes the clubs had more whites than blacks. That's been the white man's pattern: keep blacks in their own section and as soon as we start making music and entertainment, come flocking to our neighborhood. Night-club-goers lined up at the Paradise to see the Idlewild Revue, the Braggettes, or Joe Ziggy's Revue. The Paradise and the Flamingo were open all week during the summer and in the fall for deer season. On the weekends these two clubs were so crowded that cars were lined up on U.S. 10 all the way to Idlewild.

I never booked shows at Idlewild because I didn't want to work where I had my fun. I sent some of my Forest Club acts up to the Fiesta Room, including jazz singing great Betty "Bebop" Carter. Betty first sang at the Forest Club in the late 1940s. On one occasion in the 1950s I had the Ink Spots drive Betty Carter up to the club. I was kind of sweet on Betty Carter. After she arrived, I went over to see her show. I told her, "I'll be waiting outside for you after the show." She politely said, "I already have a date tonight." Joe Ziggy found out my intentions and came over and started poking fun at me. He slyly informed me, "Get out of the saddle, boy. You ain't riding anymore tonight." I didn't know Ziggy had already stolen her away.

Up at Idlewild Ziggy and I would challenge each other to dance contests. We might be in a bar and the two of us would go at it. His feet were small and effeminate looking. He could really move in his number-four dance shoes. I could outdance Ziggy, but I couldn't match his skills as a producer. He was a talented man and I loved him like a brother.

On one occasion Joe Ziggy and I brought an act from Idlewild down to the Forest Club. At the El Morocco, I heard a fine little group led by a saxophonist. This fella had a sad, mournful sound that cut right through me. Joe Ziggy was sitting with me and I asked him, "Do you think the folks down in Detroit would go for this group?" Ziggy answered, "They sound good to me." I then invited the sax man and his group to play at the Forest Club. Since they weren't in the union, I arranged to get them into the local and had them sign a six-week contract. One evening I got a call from Joe Ziggy at the club.

"Sunnie, man, we're really in trouble," warned Ziggy.

I asked, "What's the matter, man?"

"You hired this band and they can't read a note of music."

Back then, all the chorus-line and shake-dancers' music was orchestrated on paper to accompany the dance routines. I was in deep; I had a six-week contract with a band that couldn't read a damn thing on the charts. As luck would have it, the leader was behind on his payments on the band's truck and it was confiscated with all the instruments inside. Desperate to get the band's equipment back, the leader struck a deal with me. He told me that if I gave him a few hundred dollars, he would forget all about the six-week engagement. I handed him the money and he went on his way. Fortunately, it worked out for both us. The sax man got his van back and that couple of hundred dollars was a hell of a lot cheaper than hiring a musical instructor to teach those boys how to read the charts and arrangements.

At Idlewild I met a number of fine musicians like saxophonist and arranger Dr. Thomas "Beans" Bowles, a fine reed player, flutist, and later the musical director at Motown Records. His wife, whom I had already known for some time, introduced me to him. She was a beautiful person who helped Beans throughout his career. After I heard him perform, I booked him to play at the Forest Club. He played at my place with a pianist out of New York, Mack McCrary, in McCrary's All-stars, which included the great instrumentalist Yusef Lateef. Later, he left the Forest Club and went over to the Flame Show Bar.

Though it became known for its nighttime entertainment, Idlewild was a family vacation spot. Idlewild Lake is a very deep, spring-fed lake. Idlewild's beach is one of only two public beaches in Yates Township. On hot afternoons, during the heyday of the resort, the beach was packed. I remember how Reverend Brady, pastor of Detroit's Second Baptist Church, used to walk down on the beach and scold the young people for wearing their bathing suits. "You're half-naked here. Get some clothes on!" he'd shout.

Back in its heyday Idlewild offered an array of activities. Phil Giles rented paddle boats and offered excursion boats that took you around the lake. Open Wooden Century speedboats dotted the lakes with fishermen and vacationers. Every season, Idlewilders held a regatta to show off all the beautifully decorated boats. I enjoyed taking out a small boat alone and rowing across the lake, taking my time to absorb its beauty and serenity.

Apart from water sports, Idlewild offered horseback riding too. Sergeant Johnson, an old army veteran, ran a riding stable that had several fine riding horses. He always wore his cavalry riding pants, boots, and army hat. Known to the locals as Sarge, Sergeant Johnson took the children on group rides around the lake. The young folks just loved Sergeant Johnson.

As it increasingly attracted everyday vacationers, Idlewild continued to be the summer home to wealthy and influential black individuals—a number of prominent African Americans like Dr. Lorenzo Nelson, Attorney Craigen, and Congressman William Dawson of Chicago. A big, fine-looking man, Dr. Nelson had a tremendous medical practice in Idlewild. Before his death he purchased a great deal of land and establishments. His wife and daughter, America, still own a great deal of property. Senator Charles Roxborough was a regular. His nephew Charles "Sonny" Roxborough opened the Rosana and still resides in Idlewild. Even one of Louis Armstrong's last wives bought a place on the island.

While vacationing in Idlewild I met a young woman, Miss Brown. She was a registered nurse and the daughter of Doctor Brown, a dermatologist who owned a place on the lake. Most of her family was dark-skinned. Her light complexion made her an outcast with most of her siblings. They didn't want too much to do with her. Dr. Brown liked me. When he fell ill, he told me to take care of his daughter. After he and his wife died, Miss Brown inherited everything. Not long after, Miss Brown and I planned to be married. Unknown to me, she had breast cancer. All the time we courted, she kept her sickness a secret. While she was ill in the hospital, she gave me the deeds to the family's land in Idlewild. After she died, I did not believe I had any right to the land, so I gave the deeds back to her brother. She was a beautiful woman.

Though I never owned land in Idlewild, I will always feel a deep connection with its development. In 1954 I financed the purchase of the Detroit Idlewilders clubhouse from a doctor out of Chicago. Afterward, I turned it over to the organization. Each Detroit member owns a share of the clubhouse. Over the years, noted members of Detroit Idlewilders have included Charles Diggs Jr., Hobart Taylor, Dr. Robert Bennett, and pioneer businesswoman Maxine Powell. Before joining the staff of Motown Records as director of the company's artist and development finishing school in 1964, Ms. Powell founded the Maxine Powell Finishing School, Detroit's first black-owned modeling business. A year later, she acquired Ferry Center at 275 E. Ferry, a nice spot that she rented for dances, weddings, meetings, and the like. In 1955 Ms. Powell got her first big modeling contract with Pontiac Motors. Dr. Bennett and I attended the event. Later she acquired contracts with Packard and Chrysler. Until she sold the center in 1964, Ms. Powell often provided Ferry Center as the Detroit Idlewilders meeting spot.

The early 1960s still saw a great deal of musical activity at Idlewild. Under the production skills of Joe Ziggy, Bragg's 1961 Idlewild Revue featured singers Arthur Prysock, Roy Hamilton, organist Bill Doggett, and comedian George Kirby. The following year's lineup starred T-Bone Walker, Della Reese, Lavern Baker, and Dakota Staton. Another featured act at Idlewild, the Four Tops were a group of talented young men. Originally called the Four Aims, they had toured and recorded since the mid 1950s. After signing with Motown in 1963, they found fame and a worldwide audience.

The 1964 Civil Rights Act, which struck down segregation, took its toll on Idlewild. After 1964, blacks began to flock to Florida beach resorts and the gambling casinos of Las Vegas, leaving Idlewild behind. By the late 1960s, entertainers at the Flamingo and the Fiesta Room were playing to scant audiences, and the Casa Blanca Hotel was converted into a childcare center.

By the early 1970s, the Flamingo remained open periodically and the Paradise stayed open only four nights a week. Several years ago, snow caved in the roof of the Paradise and the building was torn down. The Flamingo finally closed due to the failure to pay back taxes. The club is still standing, but it is being sighted for use as a youth recreational center.

No city or county can survive for long without a built-in economy. When the doors of establishments began to open all over America, blacks left Idlewild behind. All the prosperity and sense of community in Idlewild and Paradise faded away, leaving the economy in a dismal state. According to current statistics, Idlewild has the highest number of welfare recipients in Michigan.[8] I apologize if I offend my black brothers and sisters, but the truth must be told. The blame for this decline cannot be put on "them," for it was we who were responsible for Idlewild's decline. The majority of the houses one sees there today were built over fifty years ago; many are now abandoned or in ill repair. When I was president of the Idlewilders, I assembled lawyers and worked to secure Federal Housing Authority grants to improve housing. We gave back to Lake County.

Idlewild is a ghost town trying to reclaim itself. Little has changed since the exodus of some thirty years ago. There are some signs of progress, however. I helped open a small black-owned store in Idlewild. Across the street from the store, Mr. William McClure, a retired jazz nightclub owner from Indianapolis, opened the Red Rooster Lounge and is featuring jazz and blues acts from around the state.

Recently, I met Vivian and Charles Webb from Southfield, Michigan, who purchased the Jones house. I told them the history of the residence and they are planning to restore it to its original state. Mrs. Webb first came to Idlewild with her parents when she was fifteen. Though her husband had never heard of Idlewild, he agreed to take a ride there. Just like so many before him, he fell in love with the place. In a letter to me Mrs. Webb wrote, "We love Idlewild—its trees, its lakes, and its tranquility. My husband

---

8. According to 1990 census figures, 37 percent of Lake County's children live in poverty.

doesn't complain about the distance now; he can't wait to get there and hates to leave. It is our peaceful paradise."

Idlewild will always remain one of my most cherished memories. Today our original Detroit club has grown into five chapters, representing members from Detroit, Cleveland, St. Louis, and two from Chicago. I still serve as president emeritus of the Idlewilders. Every year in August the various chapters meet for a week of festivities in Idlewild. Though the resort remains busy until Labor Day, the Idlewilder clubs have traditionally ended their activities with this yearly get-together. This week-long celebration has always climaxed with an annual fashion show. In Idlewild's heyday the show brought in models from Chicago.

When I returned from this event in the summer of 1995, I was pleased to learn that the Detroit television special, *Idlewild, A Place in the Sun,* had aired during my absence. This program brought a great deal of new interest and publicity to Idlewild. After my return home, my phone rang constantly with young people inquiring about the resort—about the historic acquisition of land, its famous residents, and the renting of cottages. I encouraged these young folks, as I encourage all other young black folks, to reinvest in Idlewild, to visit and to keep the dream of its African American founders alive.

◆ 7 ◆
Every Day Is a New Story

A lthough Sunnie Wilson continued to travel with Joe Louis in the 1950s, he witnessed vast changes in his life and in Detroit. As Wilson explained, "If you live as long as I have, you're bound to see things change around you. It's part of the plan." When Wilson first arrived in Detroit, Ford Model Ts and streetcars carried passengers along crowded streets. During the Depression, Wilson broke into show business, dancing and leading show bands, sometimes earning two or three dollars a night. As the country entered World War II, he found prosperity as a nightclub and hotel owner.

The postwar years, however, wrought massive changes in the city—changes that affected not only Wilson's life and business, but those of thousands of Detroiters. Mayor Edward Jeffries' 1946 Detroit Plan selected Black Bottom as the number-one site for slum clearance. When the Detroit Plan was issued in its final form in 1951, 140,000 blacks lived in Black Bottom. Soon many middle-class blacks moved to the more prominent neighborhoods of La Salle Boulevard, Chicago Boulevard, Boston-Edison, and Arden Park. Displacement from Black Bottom led many economically disadvantaged blacks to take up residence around Twelfth Street, the former Jewish "second front" on the city's northwest side—a section that unfortunately never engendered the favorable climate of community known to former east-side residents.

147

In 1959 bulldozers tore into the earth around Hastings Street, creating a deep, earthen trench to accommodate the I-75 freeway. Along with the destruction of the former east-side community, integration saw the decline of black business. Following the Supreme Court's 1954 decision, integration began to break down the barriers separating black and white entrepreneurs and consumers. Initially hopeful that integration would stimulate the growth of black business, the expectations of African American entrepreneurs like Wilson were cut short. One of Wilson's early business associates, drugstore-chain owner Sidney Barthwell, commented that, "Negroes had it made in Detroit until World War II. We had about everything we needed in the black business community. Discrimination gave us tremendous [economic] power because we had been compacted in one small area."[1] As Wilson explained, "We thought integration would be a two-way street, that a partnership between black and white business would evolve, but it didn't turn out that way."

In November, during the 1952 presidential election, President Harry S Truman embarked on a cross-country speaking campaign in support of Democratic presidential candidate Adlai Stevenson, the progressive governor of Illinois. After numerous attempts by President Truman and others to persuade Stevenson to run, the Illinois governor finally accepted the Democratic nomination to run against Republican candidate Dwight D. Eisenhower. A few weeks before President Truman's visit to Michigan, he appeared before a crowd of two hundred thousand black folks in Harlem. The president was scheduled to speak in Detroit and the nearby city of Hamtramck—the city's Polish enclave. I then became involved in an effort to bring the president into Detroit's black neighborhood. I, along with a number of Negro businessmen and women—including Ms. Lillian Hatcher, Attorney Harold Bledsoe, Emmitt Cunningham, and Dr. Bob Bennett—attended meetings at the Mark Twain and a convention center to arrange for the president to stop at a park on John R and

1. Quoted in Scott McGhee and Susan Watson, eds., *Blacks in Detroit: A Reprint of Articles from the Detroit Free Press* (Detroit: Detroit Free Press, 1980), 61.

Medbury on his way downtown to visit Grand Circus Park and Washington Boulevard.

President Truman arrived in Highland Park at the Grand Trunk Station on his personal train car, the Ferdinand Magellan, the same train car in which he had visited Detroit during his famous 1948 whistle-stop tour. The white city officials in Hamtramck opposed the president's visit to the black neighborhood, claiming that the black folks would pose a threat to his life. I informed them that the president would face greater danger in Hamtramck because down in Paradise Valley the black folks just loved him.

Our group worked day and night and drew a hell of a crowd. The day of the event, the president, his daughter Margaret, and Governor Williams visited Hamtramck's Veterans' Memorial Hospital and then passed open factory windows filled with supporters as they proceeded to our scheduled stop at John R and Medbury. The president, his daughter, and Governor Williams stepped from their open motor car and mounted a stage in the park, from which the president addressed a crowd of predominantly black Democratic supporters. In his brief address the president reiterated his contribution to desegregating the armed forces. On his way to the Sheraton-Cadillac Hotel, he visited Grand Circus Park and Washington Boulevard.

I helped coordinate the event from a car phone in my convertible Pontiac. I had been up all night and didn't have a chance to get home to dress for the occasion, so I sat in my Pontiac, wearing slacks and a red sweater. Mr. Truman's 1952 tour marked the first time a president campaigned in the black neighborhoods. Today I remain grateful to all those who helped me organize the president's appearance. And we all will never forget Mr. Truman's respect for the black community. Later, I received a letter from him, thanking me for my contribution.

Though the Democrats met defeat against the Republican ticket of Eisenhower and Nixon in 1952, I resumed my entrepreneurial activities by setting out to create a gathering spot for my patrons at the Mark Twain. I brought my Forest Club B license over to the hotel and opened a new downstairs cocktail lounge, the Swamp Room. The Mark Twain's downstairs lounge had one of the prettiest bars in the country. I had a nice jukebox and adorned the room with potted palm trees. On one wall I had a mural of a Louisiana swamp with moss-covered trees rising out of the water. The lounge featured the Chicken Shack's famous white piano and everybody played on it, from Duke Ellington to Nat King Cole. In the early 1950s pianist Hugh Lawson and bassist Ernie Farrow[2] performed as a duo for Sunday sessions in the Swamp Room. Later in the decade, pianist-saxophonist Teddy Harris led a five-piece band at the Swamp Room.

During the early 1950s, saxophone giant Lester "The Prez" Young stayed at my place. He often came to town with Norman Granz's Jazz at the Philharmonic series, which featured a great lineup of talent. The Prez didn't say much to anyone. He'd go up to his room with his scotch and horns and lock his door. He'd lay around his room and play his horn until it was time to go to his gig.

Texas-born blues guitarist T-Bone Walker became another regular at the Mark Twain. A skinny fella, T-Bone was a lovable guy who could really play the guitar. He stayed at my place when he was performing at Raymond "Sportree" Jackson's Sportree Reed's Bar at Hastings and Adams, or the Frolic.

One time T-Bone Walker stayed in the lucky suite and threw a big party. While he was busy drinking and entertaining his guests, someone stole his watch and ring. Enraged, he began cussing everybody out in the room. Later, a fella called and told T-Bone that his girlfriend had picked up the watch and ring. This fella brought the stolen items to T-Bone's room. I humorously reminded T-Bone, who was still very mad, "You should be very thankful. If you'd been staying in another room, you would have never got those things back."

Among the many musicians who checked in at my place was trumpeter Dizzy Gillespie. He stayed, until one day I went to his room and couldn't find him anywhere. He had left without a word. Dizzy was a fine young man, but a little hard to figure out

2. Hugh Lawson and Ernie Farrow later appeared at the Blue Bird Inn and became members of Yusef Lateef's band, recording many records for the Savoy label.

sometimes. Walking down the street a few days later, I passed a restaurant, and in the front window I saw Dizzy having lunch with drummer J. C. Heard. I didn't blame Dizzy for preferring the company of another musician, especially a talent like J. C. Heard. Yet I still felt a little jealous that J. C. had made off with my tenant. So I went into the place and walked up to the table where Dizzy and J. C. were sitting. "Hello, J. C.," I said addressing Mr. Heard without looking at Dizzy. "I need a favor from you."

"What do you need, Mr. Wilson?" asked J. C.

"I'd like to learn to play the drums," I told him.

"What? Sunnie, you're a businessman. You don't really want to play the drums," he said, a little amused at my request.

I repeated resolutely, "I want to learn to play the drums."

"Listen, Sunnie, I don't have the time, and besides you. . . ."

"No, I want you to teach me."

"Why?" asked J. C., who was starting to get annoyed by my prodding.

"Because if I learn to play the drums," I answered, "I can get my old tenant back." Then we all burst out laughing.

Dizzy wasn't the only one to leave my place without paying his bill. Down through the years, musicians must have given me a bushel basket full of bad checks and IOUs. Until this day, singer Etta James and her mother still owe me nine hundred dollars. When comedian Mantan Moreland came to town to play the Flame Show Bar with his partner Bud Harris in the 1950s, he didn't have enough money to get back on the road. Mantan found his fame in the old Charlie Chan films. I put him up at the Mark Twain. One day the desk clerk told me, "Your friend Mantan is racking up an exorbitant bill." I told the clerk, "Don't worry. I'm going to have a talk with my guest." I confronted Mantan and said, "Mantan, they tell me you're running up quite a bill, that you're on that phone all day. I just can't cover your bills."

Instead of showing any sign of apprehension or concern, Mantan gushed with excitement. "Man, I was just thinking about you," he said. Wary of his intentions, I asked, "What do you mean, man?" "Let's get an act together," he answered.

People have tried to buy me off with all sorts of things, but

151

I never had someone attempt to pay his bills by offering me a part in a stage act. By that time in life I had no interest in returning to the stage. Unfortunately, my friend Mantan never showed much interest in paying his tab. Years later I'd see Mantan some place, and he'd say, "I'm still writing that script for us."

Not all of my guests slipped out so easy, however. One day a delivery truck pulled up to the hotel. The drivers saw the rear end and two legs of a big fat man hanging out a first-floor window. The delivery men came in and told me a man was caught in one of my windows and was hollering for help. This man was a blues singer, a big heavy fella. I knew he was trying to skip out on his tab because the drivers had seen his bags lying on the ground outside the window. When I entered the room, I saw the front half of this man with the window resting on top of his huge frame.

"Mr. Wilson, please get me out. The window fell down on me."

I slowly inspected the situation, taking my time as the man hung painfully over the windowsill.

"What are you doing in that window?" I asked. "You weren't trying to leave without paying, were you?"

"Oh no, Mr. Wilson."

"Does it hurt?" I asked.

"Yes, Mr. Wilson. Please get me out of here."

"Well if you're hurt, then maybe I ought to call the police."

"No, no, Mr. Wilson, don't call the police," pleaded the man.

"Give me my money then," I demanded.

"Yes sir, Mr. Wilson, I'll get your money."

I then got a few people together outside, and we pulled the man out of the window. I made him walk around the building and enter the front door. Sensing this fella was getting upset, I said a few humorous words and made him laugh. Then I made him promise to pay me.

But for the most part my guests never made trouble, especially those from the gospel music world, guests like the Five Blind Boys, the Daisy Sisters, the Clouds of Joy, Pearl Bailey, and Sister Rosetta Tharpe. Miss Tharpe was a religious singer, but when times got bad on the road, she would resort to performing in jazz houses and cabarets. During the holidays, these singers would perform live on the radio. One Easter morning Rosetta Tharpe and T-Bone Walker joined a number of the gospel singers in a impromptu session in the second-floor lobby. They brought down guitars and horns. The harmonies were the most beautiful sound I've ever heard.

The Reverend C. L. Franklin, father of singing star Aretha Franklin, used to stay at my place on occasion. In the early days before he became famous, he had the Bethel Baptist Church on Hastings. I used to loan him chairs from the Forest Club. He'd come and get them on Sunday and return them Monday morning. Joe Von Battle, owner of Joe's Record Shop on Hastings Street, recorded Franklin's sermons at Bethel Baptist Church and leased the recordings to Chess records in Chicago. They became million-sellers. Although Franklin had an ego, I got along with him. We used to drink together and jokingly taunt each other. I liked to get him riled up. I would start by saying, "I could make you a big man." He'd respond with, "You can't make me a big man. I'm already a big man."

After his boastful announcement, I would keep up the contest. "I got to make you a big man, because you can't sing and you can't preach." By then he would start to get upset. "Goddamn it, I'm a big man and you're just a little man!" Then I would stop him, and calmly say, "See that—that's what I mean. You're always trying to prove you're big. I can help you, fella." We would go on and on with this.

What I liked about Reverend Franklin is that even after he began to make it big, he still took time out to hone his skills as an orator. I respected the fact that the Reverend Franklin believed he had more to learn. He studied under another reverend who taught him how to preach. Reverend Franklin sent for this man and put him up in my hotel. They held regular sessions. Soon Reverend Franklin began to sound just like this man. He adopted the same low inflections and vocal rises.

By the 1950s, many up-and-coming names in the music world were guests at the Mark Twain. When Nat King Cole came back to play a big show on Grand River, he brought a forty-piece orchestra with him and they all stayed at my place. Another guest, singer Bobby Bland, became the hotel's honorary steward. When I stepped out or had business out of town, he damn near ran the place.

B. B. King stayed at the Mark Twain. While performing at a downtown theater, he related that he had no money to put up his band. Learning of his predicament, a shoe-shine man approached B. B. backstage and told him to contact Sunnie Wilson at the Mark Twain Hotel. I put up B. B.'s band and the next morning fed every member. B. B. and I became great friends and he has never forgotten the help I gave him. Whenever he came to town, he'd come by to see me. Years later, in 1976, I promoted a show for him at the Windsor Arena in Canada.

During the 1950s, the most prestigious black-owned hotel was the Gotham at 111 Orchestra Place. Known from coast to coast, the Gotham was designed by renowned architect Albert Kahn, and built by white businessman Albert B. Hartz in 1925 at a cost of $590,000. A nine-story establishment, the Gotham boasted three hundred rooms decorated with plush carpeting and solid mahogany furniture. The hotel's Ebony Dining Room served excellent food. Since the Mark Twain only had a snack bar, my associates and I ate our meals at the Gotham, which was within walking distance of my hotel. The Gotham's chef, Mr. Madison, outclassed the cook at the Book Cadillac Hotel. He made beautiful ice sculptures that adorned the fine cloth-covered tables.

Among the Gotham's noted African American guests were poet Langston Hughes, Congressman Adam Clayton Powell, and singer Billie Holiday. At the Gotham I met a young Sammy Davis Jr. when he stayed at the hotel with his family. Some whites came to the Gotham, but their numbers were limited because they had their own places downtown.

In 1943 two black businessmen, Mr. Hammonds and Irving Roane, bought the Gotham. When Mr. Hammonds left the business, he gave his half of the partnership to John White. Down the line, Mr. White bought out Mr. Roane's interest and became the Gotham's sole proprietor. An Ohio-born black gentleman, John White came to Detroit in the 1920s and made important contributions to the community and the Urban League. At one time, Mr. White was the city's leading numbers-man. Many of the gangsters picked up their numbers from him.

For years the Gotham stood as a proud example of black entrepreneurship. The Gotham housed the Gotham Social Club, which included members such as Eddie Cummings and Mr. Safford, prominent black Detroiters who ran numbers units. Mr. Cummings and Mr. Safford were the founders of a prestigious black resort in Ontario, Canada. In 1949 Mr. Cummings took his son with him to investigate a lot that was for sale in Rochester Township, Ontario. After his car got stuck on a gravel road, a local farmer informed him about a large parcel of lakeside farmland for sale outside of Belle River. Taking notice of the valuable lakefront acreage, he contacted several other black Detroiters to purchase the land. With five thousand dollars of his own money, Mr. Cummings brought together nineteen other investors and formed Belle Claire Shores Limited, and its nonprofit affiliate, the Surf Club. The land included a well-kept, two-story house and almost one mile of beach fronting Lake St. Claire.

In 1952 Eddie Cummings and Mr. Safford financed the building of a clubhouse for the Surf Club at a cost of $250,000. The Surf Club came to be managed by Burrell "Junior" Pace, who built a home on the Canadian side. Dr. Walter "Squawk" Harmon built a home there and so did Dr. Preston. Members gave Joe Louis some land, but he gave it to Dr. Bennett. During his comeback attempt in 1950, Joe trained at the Surf Club, running on the road that stretched between Belle River and Stoney Point. For years, wealthy blacks bought homes on the Canadian side. The Surf Club also had several private hotels where members and their guests could stay for the weekend. The locals were very supportive of the club and its visitors because it brought substantial money to the area. Blacks who owned boats sailed from Detroit to dine at the Surf Club. Because the Surf Club was located on a wetlands area connected by a low-lying channel, boaters docked on the river and traveled a short distance to the clubhouse.

The club didn't feature big entertainment. It held modeling shows by Detroit-based Howard and his Little Foxes. Sometimes it had a pianist or Joe Ziggy's group. But for the most part, the club remained a dining establishment.

If people wanted top-notch entertainment, they could still find a vibrant jazz music scene in Detroit. During the 1950s there were clubs all over the city—places like the Flame Show Bar on John R, the Blue Bird Inn on Tireman, the Twenty Grand on Grand River, and Klein's on Twelfth Street. There were a number of small lounges that featured pianists and small combos. They had piano players at the Carlton Plaza Hotel and the 606 Horseshoe Lounge on Adams.

At that time, I brought a number of small combos into the Swamp Room at the Mark Twain. I hired a number of women musicians like Miss Hadda Brooks, the Queen of the Boogie. A fine singer and pianist, Hadda made some outstanding recordings on the Los Angeles–based Modern label and made musical appearances in two Hollywood films—*In a Lonely Place* starring Humphrey Bogart and *The Bad and the Beautiful* with Kirk Douglas and Lana Turner. She played her first Detroit gig at the Flame in 1952; a few years later I brought her to my place.[3]

I have always been drawn to the sound of the piano. My local piano talents at the Swamp Room included Don Hill and Faye Thomas. Most of the time the women outplayed the men. Faye sang in the style of Billie Holiday. She would play all night long; when the musicians who sat in got tired, she would send someone upstairs to get more.

---

3. Hadda Hapgood was born the daughter of John Hapgood, a deputy sheriff, and Goldie Wright, a dentist, in Los Angeles, California, on October 29, 1916. In her youth she formally studied music with a Italian piano instructor, Florence Bruni, with whom she trained for twenty years. She attended University of Chicago, and later, after returning to Los Angeles, she attracted the attention of restaurant-owner and record-label owner Jules Bihari. Bihari, along with his brothers Joe and Saul, launched the Modern label. To find Hapgood a more suitable show name, Bihari gave her the recording name Hadda Brooks. In 1945 Brooks's instrumental hit recording "Swinging the Boogie" and her subsequent numbers financially established the Biharis' label. Brooks's career as one of the era's most talented woman singers and pianists was also launched.

156

In the 1950s I enjoyed the company of alto saxophonist Charlie Parker. He played the Forest Club on a number of occasions. For one of his performances he brought in a string section. On that particular evening he did not show for the opening and the band had to start without him. During the concert, Charlie rushed up on stage and, without putting on the strap on his saxophone, blew the rest of the set by holding the bottom of his horn. Whenever Charlie Parker came to Detroit, he looked me up at one of my places. We made the rounds, drinking and talking together at blind pigs. Not long after one of our nights on the town, I got a call from New York in March of 1955 that he had died. His people asked if I would help to organize his funeral. They were under the impression that I was a very close friend. I informed them that unfortunately, I could not help them. They eventually buried him in his hometown of Kansas City. I didn't know the darker side of Charlie Parker—his problems with drug addiction and the like—only that he was a beautiful gentleman and a musical genius.

When he came to Detroit in the early 1950s, Parker frequently jammed at the Blue Bird Inn. A gathering spot for local bebop musicians, the Blue Bird also featured many of the top names in modern jazz. During one of his shows at the Blue Bird Inn, organist Jimmy Smith stayed at the Mark Twain. At that time he used to travel with his organ in the back of a used hearse. When he got to my place, he parked the hearse in the front of the hotel. My customers began to ask, "Sunnie Wilson, who died at your place?" Perturbed by these inquiries, I answered, "Nobody, man!" Then I told Jimmy Smith to park that damn hearse back in the alley.

As the decade progressed, I watched the rise of two popular vocal talents: my former Golden Gloves boxer Jackie Wilson and gospel singing star Sam Cooke. I treated Sam like a son. As a teenager he appeared at the Forest Club with his first group, the Highway QCs. Later, when he was with the Soul Stirrers Sam stayed at the Mark Twain.[4] When he got off the tour bus at my

---

4. As a member of the Highway QCs, Cooke appeared at the Forest Club on Sunday, February 20, 1949, as part of a gospel-singing bat-

place, he often asked me if I could hold onto his satchel of money. "Don't you want to count it?" I'd ask. He politely responded, "Since you're holding it for me, there's no reason to count it." I put the bag under my bed. One time Sam heard I wasn't doing so well financially. He thought so much of me that he threw a party for me at the Graystone.

But while I treated Sam as my son, it was Jackie Wilson who jokingly referred to me as his father. Jackie was a tough fella who, back in his Golden Gloves days, hit his opponents hard. He eventually replaced Clyde McPhatter in the singing group the Dominoes. Later he became a star attraction at Morris Wasserman's Flame Show Bar on John R. I was amused by his reference to me as his father, until one day I passed the Flame and saw a marquee that read, "Tonight Sunnie Wilson Jr." I told Jackie, "I'm a businessman and I have a wife and family. You have to take that name off the marquee."[5]

But of all the entertainers and celebrities I kept company with during the decade, Joe Louis remained my closest friend. During those years, Joe failed at making a comeback in 1950. In 1951 he fought his last bout and suffered a humiliating defeat at the fists of Rocky Marciano. Though in financial straits, he continued to keep credibility with his public. In October 1953 Detroit Mayor Albert E. Cobo proclaimed the last week of October "Joe Louis Week." I attended a party as part of the week-long celebration in the Holiday Suite of the Gotham Hotel. Those in attendance included Mayor Cobo, John Roxborough, Freddie Guinyard, and Ma Robinson from Atlantic City.

Though his boxing career had ended, Joe experienced his worst loss in December 1953 with the death of his mother, Lillie.

---

tle which pitted the group against the St. Louis–based Harmony Kings and Detroit's Flying Clouds.

The Soul Stirrers were founded as a quartet in Trinity, Texas, in 1934. Cooke first recorded with the Soul Stirrers in 1951 and stayed with the group until 1957.

5. Located on 4264 John R. on the corner of Canfield, the Flame Show Bar opened in July 1949. For over a decade, along with its talented house band led by Maurice King, the Flame featured such noted performers as Billie Holiday, Dinah Washington, and Erroll Garner.

Joe and Lillie were extremely close. Every time they were reunited, they embraced with overflowing affection. Joe credited his mother with giving him a good path in life. As he once said, "My mother always taught me to be honest and that a good name is better than riches." When Joe lost Lillie, he felt as if he had lost his most cherished fortune.

But despite his losses and setbacks, Joe remained an amiable and positive individual. No matter where he went, we kept in close contact. In New York, we stopped in at Sugar Ray's bar on Seventh Avenue between 123rd and 124th Streets. Sugar Ray's bar became a hangout for many celebrities like Jackie Robinson, Frank Sinatra, and Lena Horne.

On Christmas Day in 1955 I attended Joe's wedding to Rose Morgan at her house in St. Albans, New York.[6] Rose Morgan owned a New York beauty salon and a cosmetics business. She was an attractive and very intelligent woman. St. Albans was a neighborhood of neatly kept homes. Count Basie, one of the first black musicians to make his home there, lived a few doors down from Rose Morgan; trumpeter Cootie Williams lived around the corner. Count volunteered to play at the ceremony. Unexpectedly, Cootie showed up with his horn and joined Count in entertaining the guests.

After the wedding my New York friends threw me a party in a suite at the Theresa Hotel. Although the room was filled with the festive atmosphere of pretty girls and champagne, I began to think of my friends, a group of fellas who gathered on Christmas Day—an informal group made up of twenty-five black men—businessmen, lawyers, and doctors. Throughout the year, we gathered monthly at members' homes to eat a nice meal, socialize, and discuss business. Most of the group lived in nice residences on Chicago, Boston Boulevard, and Arden Park. We put money in a pot and at the end of the year, we used it to finance a Christmas celebration. Our group included Attorney Harold Bledsoe, Judge James Del Rio, Dr. Robert Bennett, Dr. Guy Salisbury, Dr. Walter Harmon, Dr. Rudy Porter, and Dr. Marlow.

---

6. Joe Louis was married to Marva Louis twice—from 1935 to 1945 and from 1946 to 1949.

Dr. Marlow, a successful dentist, was our elder and we all looked up to him. Today there are only two of our group left, James Del Rio and myself.

Our group also included one of Attorney Bledsoe's former understudies, Hobart Taylor. Among our group, Hobart became the most internationally known. He was a good friend and fellow Idlewilder—an aloof man whose gentlemanly character stemmed from his Southern upbringing. A native of Texas, Hobart's father was the owner of a successful cab company and a personal friend of Lyndon B. Johnson.

Hobart came north to study law at the University of Michigan and became editor of the school's law review. Eventually he worked for Harold Bledsoe. According to some, Hobart was one the finest lawyers in the country, an intellectual giant. In 1951 he was named chief of the civil rights division of the Wayne County Prosecutor's office. When Lyndon Johnson became vice president in 1961, he appointed Hobart as a special counsel to President Kennedy's Committee on Equal Job Rights for Negroes. After President Johnson's election in 1964, he did not forget his friend Hobart Taylor and gave him a job as one his top presidential aides.

Each year, different members hosted the celebration at their homes. At midnight on Christmas Eve we had what we called a midnight lunch, cooked by one of the fellas' wives. Since the bars closed early, I could always make the event. We would eat and review the year. When I was at my party at the Theresa, amid all the festivities, I began to miss my friends. Without attracting the notice of my New York hosts, I left the room and called the porter to have my bags ready in the lobby. Then I booked a flight to Detroit and arranged to have my friend, Dr. Bennett, pick me up from the airport. Back in Detroit, I made it in time to have our midnight meal. Even among the bright lights and celebrities, one cannot forget old friends. When I got to the house where the fellas were having dinner, they all greeted me like a long lost soul.

After Joe's wedding to Rose Morgan, he and I continued to travel together. We often took a boat from Miami to Cuba. Only ninety miles off the Florida coast, Cuba had everything you wanted. I liked it much better than Nassau, Bahamas. It had beautiful, clean beaches, friendly people, and attractive women whose lives were absorbed in nature and the rhythm of song. We stayed at splendid places like the Riviera and the Hotel Nacionnal. The poor folks of small countries like Cuba welcomed vacationers because the foreigners would give them money on the street. When I was a small boy in South Carolina, my friends and I would wait for the number-one train on its way to Florida. As it passed we yelled out, "Scramble! Scramble!" and the white passengers would throw money out the window. Then we'd scramble to dig the coins out of the dirt alongside the tracks. Likewise, the Cuban people welcomed us and treated us very well.

Cuban President Fulgencio Batista liked Joe, too. We used to meet him in Havana. Through the connections of actor George Raft, Joe planned to open a nightclub in Havana. To start a business in Havana at that time, you had to go through a Cuban. So with the help of Joe's old friend George Raft, we met with President Batista to complete the deal. This was shortly before Castro took over Cuba in 1959. A great admirer of Joe, Batista returned Joe's money, explaining that the venture would be jeopardized by the increasing trouble in the country. The next I heard, President Batista had left the country for Spain with all his associates' money.

As the cold war and the threat of Communist expansion was transforming countries like Cuba, back home in Detroit, the city was undergoing its own changes. Hastings Street, once crowded with nightclub-goers and white patrons, no longer resembled the street of previous decades. Desegregation prompted blacks to take their money to white businesses. White nightclub-goers no longer had to go to the black neighborhoods to see a black jazz group or stage act.

By 1959 Paradise Valley became a victim of "slum clearance," or what became known as urban renewal. On the east side, big-money interests like Mr. Webster and the J. L. Hudson family bought up parcels of land. To make way for the I-75 freeway, the city decimated Black Bottom and Paradise Valley.

Along with the famous places of the east side, the Gotham

Hotel faced destruction, too. In 1962 the neighboring medical center offered to buy the Gotham. The hospital offered $350,000, but its owner John White wanted $450,000 and a fierce disagreement ensued. With the eventual consummation of the deal, the hotel was slated for demolition.

In August 1962, Joe Ziggy, one of the Gotham's longtime tenants, wrote that "After living with a person like John White for more than twenty years, it's going to be pretty hard to adjust myself to other surroundings. Closing of the Gotham won't be a picnic either. For what had been considered the best Negro owned hotel in the country, will be no more. Some of the greatest and finest people in the world have been guests in the Gotham, and I don't think there will ever be another hotel, Negro-owned, and personally managed that will come close to what John J. White established for Detroit and world visitors."[7]

In early September 1962, I, along with several hundred others, attended a farewell party held at the Gotham. Over the next several months John White sold most of the hotel's furniture. Mr. Randolph Wallace of the Garfield Hotel bought most of it. When a hotel's license is terminated, the law states that all activities in the hotel must cease. The police were aware that certain individuals were still conducting business in the hotel. On Friday, November 16, at 5:00 P.M., U.S. Treasury agents, under the command of Anthony Getto of the IRS Intelligence Division, conducted a numbers raid on the Gotham. It has always been my experience that when the police raid a hotel, they customarily carry a warrant that states which room they will search. This was not the case with the Gotham raid. Though the Detroit police had informed the agents that a pass-key was available at the hotel's desk, the agents entered the building with sledgehammers and axes. Once inside, they went on an hour-long spree, smashing down every door in the building and destroying furniture without concern for private property. John White and forty-two

---

7. Ziggy Johnson, "Zaggin' with Ziggy," *Michigan Chronicle,* August 11, 1962, p. 2.

others were arrested and charged in Recorder's Court. The day after the raid, I went down to the Gotham and couldn't believe my eyes. It was hard to believe that the authorities could commit such wanton destruction.

Through the promises of certain individuals, John White had been under the impression that he could move his numbers operation into Randolph Wallace's Garfield Hotel and Garfield Lounge, on John R. He did not know, however, that another numbers operator already had a monopoly on the Garfield. John called me and asked if he could move into the Mark Twain. I told him if all I owned was a twin bed, he could have half of it. He was a courteous man who helped those around him. He liked to laugh and loved life.

I gave him a suite on the first floor. His men brought by his furniture and belongings. So he would not use my line, I installed a pay station in the lobby—his own phone from which he could conduct his business. John told me, "Mr. Wilson, here's three hundred dollars. It's all I have. If I live, I'll make you rich; if I die, I'll owe you." He stayed with me quite a while. The white operators would come by and give him money. Sometimes I borrowed his big Lincoln.

For a time, the Gotham became a rooming house for nurses before it was destroyed by the wrecking ball in July 1963. The day they tore it down, hundreds turned out to pay their last respects to the Gotham. That day John asked me to drive him by the Gotham. When I looked over at his face, John had tears running down his cheeks. John had tuberculosis; he fell sick for eighteen months and finally died at age fifty-five in July 1964.

The destruction of the Gotham symbolized the end of an era. As the Gotham disappeared, along with countless landmarks of Detroit black history, city planners turned much of the east side into vacant lots. Without monetary power, the residents of Black Bottom were forced out and given places to live around Twelfth Street and other outlying sections. Just like other cities around the country that sought to rid themselves of run-down black neighborhoods, the takeover of Paradise Valley could not be stopped. That's been the white man's philosophy—to move in, move the people out, and let the property sit vacant. The mayor and the social services find you somewhere to live. The people who lived in the vicinity of Black Bottom—around Chene and McDougal—had very little money. Even if they wanted to protest against urban renewal, they didn't have the funds to hire the proper attorneys. Today a great portion of the east side still remains undeveloped and barren. I thought the takeover was wrong, but sometimes you can't fight "progress," especially when you are poor and your adversary is armed with the power of millions of dollars.

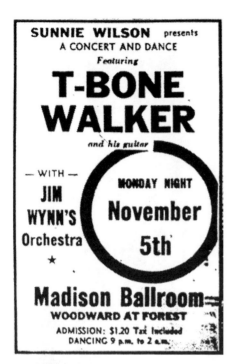

SUNNIE WILSON presents
A CONCERT AND DANCE
Featuring

T-BONE WALKER

and his guitar

— WITH —
JIM WYNN'S Orchestra
★

MONDAY NIGHT
November 5th

Madison Ballroom
WOODWARD AT FOREST
ADMISSION: $1.20 Tax Included
DANCING 9 p.m. to 2 a.m.

After the sale of the Forest Club, I continued to book acts like my friend and hotel guest T-Bone Walker, the famous blues guitarist from Texas.

"Queen of the Boogie," Hadda Brooks was one of the Swamp Room performers during the 1950s.

With Lottie the Body and drummer Chico Hamilton (right) at the Swamp Room, still trying to learn the drums.

Backstage with singer Billy Eckstine and Detroit newspaper writer Bill Lane.

Having a handshake with middleweight boxing champion Sugar Ray Robinson.

THE GOTHAM HOTEL
200 Rooms All With Bath, Tub or Shower—Popular Priced Restaurant
BOB ROBINSON, Manager

111 Orchestra Place   TE. 1-0600   Detroit (1), Michigan

From 1943 to 1962, Detroit's Gotham Hotel existed as one of the finest black-owned hotels in the country.

At the Gotham
Hotel with
owner John
White (left).

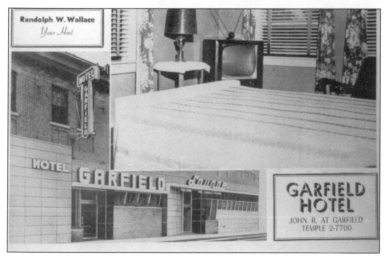

Randolph Wallace's Hotel Garfield on John R. (c. 1947).

Located near Belle River, Canada, the Surf Club (founded in 1952) existed as a Detroit black-owned hotel recreation spot.

With my dear friend Jackie Gleason, a man with unbounded talent and the owner of a golden heart.

Backstage at the Masonic
Temple with my good
friend Mr. B. B. King.

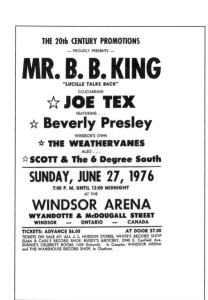

In 1976 I promoted a show in
Canada for B. B. King.

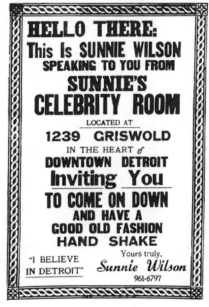

In 1974 I opened up Sunnie Wilson's
Celebrity Room downtown.

The Celebrity Room. (Photo by Darien Nemer.)

Just a few of the guests to honor me with their presence at my 80th golden anniversary celebration at the Latin Quarter: Court of Appeals Judge Myron Wahls (left) and then Michigan Supreme Court Judge Dennis Archer.

Greeting famed novelist James Baldwin during his visit to Detroit in January 1982.

Mayor Dennis Archer providing a few words during my belated birthday celebration in July 1995. (Photo by Darien Nemer.)

Surrounded by good friends at my 1995 birthday celebration. My cherished girlfriend Margaret Samples (left), Father William Cunningham of Focus Hope (center), and Lottie the Body (far right). (Photo by Darien Nemer.)

• 8 •
Let It Roll!

Following the relocation of east-side black families to Twelfth Street and other sections, Wilson witnessed the emergence of a younger generation that lacked a sense of community and family life. Without the employment opportunities of the previous decades, many of these younger black Detroiters faced disillusionment and the lure of hard drugs unknown to earlier black residents. This new breed, as Wilson refers to them, embodied a street-hardened attitude that was prone to violence and disregard for property. Many of these young people, confronted with police brutality and unemployment, expressed their despair and frustration in the wanton destruction of property during the 1967 riot.

In the next two decades, as Wilson struggled to make a living in the city's changing business climate, Wilson witnessed the passing of several of his greatest friends. Amid these changes, Wilson entered the new era, as did all others, hopeful and willing to make a difference in the lives of friends and fellow Detroiters. Today his public expression "Let it roll!" continues to convey his main philosophical premise: to strive toward achieving higher endeavors.

In 1963, as homes and famous establishments of Detroit's east side disappeared, the civil rights movement culminated in mass protests across the South, in cities like Selma, Alabama, and in rural areas of Mississippi. At that time, Detroit was host to a number of benefit shows at the Fox Theater and other venues to raise money for the NAACP.

The NAACP contacted me and asked me if I would help them raise some funds for the cause. Dr. Bennett and I agreed to promote a show. Rhythm-and-blues singer Roy Hamilton was staying at the Mark Twain and I asked him if he would like to sing at our benefit concert. He agreed. Mr. George T. Roumell, the owner of the Latin Quarter on East Grand Boulevard, let us use his hall without charge. A very dedicated Greek-born entrepreneur, Mr. Roumell started out shining shoes at the Statler Hotel and later, with the help of his father, went into the restaurant business. Over time, he established the largest catering business in the city. Mr. Roumell was very helpful. During the show he and I worked behind the bar, serving drinks to the guests.

To produce the show, I called upon Joe Ziggy. At that time Ziggy had a dance-and-music school at 301 East Warren, the Ziggy Johnson School of Theater. The school had several fine voice and dance instructors. When he lost his Idlewild gig after the Fiesta Room closed, I asked Joe Ziggy to produce our show. Along with Roy Hamilton, we had the potential to put on a hell of a show. Roy was a handsome man with a beautiful baritone voice. For the finale, Joe Ziggy had Roy sing his 1954 hit, "You'll Never Walk Alone." Singing in tribute to the spirit of the black freedom movement, Roy's rendition moved the audience to tears. The room filled with screams and cries. The audience rose from their seats and shouted, "More! More!" It remains my finest, if not the most inspiring, show I have ever promoted.

In the 1960s the city built a new freeway and the Cobo Hall convention center on the Detroit riverfront. At Cobo Hall I got involved in booking a number of shows under my 20th Century promotional company. One of my most memorable productions was a show I helped book for my good-hearted friend, Jackie Gleason. I met Mr. Gleason in Paradise Valley. He used to frequent clubs down in the Valley, including the Forest Club. Mr. Gleason befriended a local character in Paradise Valley named Broadway Joe, a natural-born con man and comedian. A native of St. Louis, Joe "Broadway" Brown came to Detroit in 1919 and worked as a theater dancer and at a local shoeshine parlor. Everybody liked Broadway Joe. He never had to buy drinks because everybody would buy them for him. Mr. Gleason liked him, too. Whenever Mr. Gleason came to town, Broadway Joe would look him up in Paradise Valley.

Mr. Gleason was a true friend, a genuine human being with a big heart. Back in the early days he looked me up when he came to town. Most people don't realize that he was a talented singer and composer. The public had a different perception of him. They thought of him strictly as a comedian and actor. But his main passion was music.

Mr. Gleason's appearance was the last show I helped promote at Cobo Hall, under 20th Century. Sponsored by the musicians' union in New York, the show was organized by my good friend and talented show producer Beverly Beltaire, who was president of P. R. Associates, a Detroit public relations firm. I helped Beverly and her husband Mark book blues and jazz concerts. Mrs. Beltaire was aware of my reputation as a successful and honest promoter and invited me to help promote Mr. Gleason's Cobo appearance. The show centered around a contest between five or six big bands. The band that best performed Mr. Gleason's theme song won a four-week, all-expenses-paid national tour. The winning band was furnished with uniforms and a tour bus.

Mr. Gleason lived in Miami Beach. The island became his entertainment headquarters when he moved his television show down to the Miami Beach Auditorium in 1964. One time while I was staying at the Holiday Inn in Miami, I called him. He asked, "Where you staying?" I told him, "Down here at the Holiday Inn." He said, "Stay where you are. Pack up your things. I'm taking you to my suite in Miami Beach." He sent a chauffeur-driven Cadillac around to take me anywhere I wanted to go. That evening his driver took me to the Fontainebleau. The Fontainebleau had two rooms, a beautiful main supper club, La Ronde, which held fifteen hundred people, and a smaller, less expensive dining room. It had two shows a night—shows that featured stars like Frank Sinatra. As Mr. Gleason's guest, I didn't have to pay a dime.

Despite my good times on the road, I began to see serious developments occurring at home. As the old era faded, the new generation was left to the streets, often at the brutal hands of the Detroit Police Department. The 1967 Detroit riot didn't surprise me. The police hadn't learned, and the black folks had become restless. During the first riot in 1943, the white people had all the guns, but by the summer of 1967, the black folks had prepared themselves for another confrontation.

Around the neighborhood of the Mark Twain, a new breed of young people walked the streets, disillusioned and violent. They had not experienced the prosperity and wealth of employment opportunities of their parents and grandparents. One Christmas Eve I was walking up to the front door of the Mark Twain when two men approached me. I said, "Merry Christmas and Happy New Year." "You better give us your money or you ain't gonna have no Merry Christmas!" threatened one of the men.

"I'm Mr. Sunnie Wilson," I said, hoping that my introduction would end their provocation. But my name meant nothing to them, and they continued to come at me. I tried to take the fella's gun. Then these two men pulled me into the alley alongside the hotel and began to beat me. They knocked me to the ground. I received blows to my head and my eye felt as though it were hanging halfway down my face. Reaching in my pocket, I finally took out my little pocket knife. When I started to act crazy, they got scared and ran. Some friends of mine finally caught up with them. I don't know the details, but they didn't rob anyone for a long time after that.

Soon I made up my mind that I could no longer do business in a section full of dope peddlers and petty criminals. As their activities increased, my business began to falter. During the early 1970s I sold my interest in the Mark Twain. A few years later the hotel was destroyed by fire.

With the hotel business waning, I had to think of a way to protect myself financially. Before putting up the Mark Twain for sale, I purchased two White Tower hamburger establishments. At one time I had an option to buy all six White Tower hamburger restaurants, but my investors eventually backed out on me. One was located on Third Street and another on Woodward near Forest, not far from the General Motors building. I got myself a white shirt, pants, apron, and cap and went to work serving hamburgers at the place on Third. I hired two employees who worked two shifts.

I was making a fairly decent living, but owning hamburger stands just wasn't my line of employment. While I was working at my stand, a black man and his wife came by and asked if I would be interested in selling it. They were Islamic. They told me they weren't interested in eating hamburgers, just selling them. "You like my place here?" I asked. The man answered, "Yes, I would like to buy it. How much do you want for it?" We settled on seventy-five thousand dollars. He paid me in cash and I used the money to pay the debts on the hotel.

I soon returned to the nightclub business. Not long after I sold the hamburger stand, I had lunch downtown with one of my associates, Attorney Robert Mitchell. Walking down Griswold Street after our meal, I spotted a place, the old Blue Note Club, with a "for lease" sign in the window. I told him, "I'm going to check into this place." Using the rest of the money from the sale of my hamburger stands, I bought the Blue Note and opened it up as Sunnie's Celebrity Room. There were no black-owned bars downtown at that time. Even in the 1970s there were some white folks who weren't pleased about having blacks opening new businesses downtown. But the businessmen in the vicinity signed for me, all except one—a foreign fella who owned a little bar nearby. Though I didn't need his signature by law to lease the club, I decided to pay him a visit anyway. Accompanied by an associate of mine, I went down to the man's bar. Taking our seats, we bought everybody in the place a drink.

The man came up and asked, "You new around here?"

"No," I said, "I just came around to ask you a question. See, I'm the fella who is leasing the club on Griswold and I just want to know why you wouldn't sign for me."

"Oh, you know how competition is. I guess I . . ."

"Well," I answered, "I'm glad to know that we're gonna be good neighbors." Nothing more was ever said between us.

With the formalities out of the way, I went to work opening up my new place. Since the Book Cadillac Hotel was across the street, my place drew a lot of celebrities, who came in after the hotel's bar closed at midnight. But it took five months to secure my downtown location. At my opening in 1974, I hired a piano player and the great jazz guitarist Grant Green. I laid out a red carpet and had a doorman. Later I booked another guitar great, Detroit-born Kenny Burrell.

One of my customers at the Celebrity Room was my long-time friend, Mayor Coleman A. Young. I first met Coleman Young in Black Bottom. Coleman was always a man on the rise. I remember when he was with the Progressive Party in 1948. He used to come to my clubs. He was a nice young man and very ambitious. During Robeson's Forest Club appearance, he served as a bodyguard with the left-wing entourage assigned to protect the guest speaker.

Some still criticize Coleman for his past politics, but I've known all sorts of people affiliated not only with the left, but actual Communists. Until his death in the fall of 1996, the revolutionary Communist and former NAACP activist Robert F. Williams sent me letters.[1] I treat my friends as individuals and consider their politics their own business.

In 1973 I contributed to Coleman's first mayoral campaign, shaking hands and working on the sound truck. I contacted singer Arthur Prysock who wrote a tune for the campaign. I lined up Diana Ross and the Four Tops to record some words in support of his campaign. They used these recordings for radio spots and sound trucks. I had my own sound truck. On one of the tapes I had Four Tops baritone singer say some laudatory words about Coleman's political agenda.

Though I supported Coleman's political career, I often dif-

---

1. As local NAACP president in Monroe, North Carolina, Robert Franklin Williams made nationwide headlines in 1959 when he stated that blacks should "meet violence with violence." Exiled from the United States after an alleged kidnapping of a white Monroe couple in 1961, Williams spent eight years abroad in Cuba and the People's Republic of China, working to establish a revolutionary black liberation front. After being taken into brief custody in London, he was granted a visa by the U.S. embassy, and re-entered the country on a special flight to Detroit in September 1969.

fered with him over his public image, namely his choice of vocabulary. I do not believe he always possessed or could find the necessary words to express himself, so he would slip into using the vocabulary of his Black Bottom roots: "goddamn," "f-you," and the like. We pick up language where we are raised. In Coleman's case, you're not talking about Shakespeare; you're talking about Black Bottom. But supplanting the proper vocabulary with profanity just didn't work to his advantage. He didn't set out to project the bad-guy image; it followed him from the place of his youth.

Unlike Coleman, Paul Robeson could fall back on different strategies in gaining his audience. If Robeson saw his crowd getting restless, he started singing. Robeson held a degree from Rutgers and Coleman was a graduate of Black Bottom. Two different men, two different voices.

After he won the election, I told Coleman I would remain his street friend, reporting to him the attitudes of the people in the community. During his years as mayor, he often came into the Celebrity Room. I remember one incident in 1985 when he ran for reelection against Tom Barrow. When he left my place, I saw Coleman go into a barbershop across the street. Tom Barrow and his people stood outside, waiting to confront him. The mayor had refused to meet Barrow in public debate.

I did not know Barrow personally. I did know that he intended to have the media capture the two in a political debate on the street. Assessing the situation, I walked across the street, made my way through the crowd, and told the mayor's people to unlock the front door. Once inside, I helped Coleman make an exit out the back door. Although we had good times together, I never could relax around the mayor while he was surrounded by his bodyguards. He had twenty-seven, all big fellas.

About the time Coleman first took office as mayor, I went to see Duke Ellington when he opened at the Michigan Theater on Bagley. I could see that Duke's health was not good. I sent a doctor to his hotel room, but he refused to see him. The next time he came to town, I sent a message saying I couldn't attend the show. The next day, he called from his hotel and asked me, "What are you doing?"

"I'm watching a picture show," I said, happy to hear his voice.

"What picture you watching?" he asked.

"A cowboy picture," I replied.

"What channel?" he inquired. Like me, Duke was crazy about westerns.

He said, "I heard you gonna open up a place downtown."

I said, "Yeah, I'm trying to open a place."

"Are you short on money. How much you need?"

"Not too short," I explained." I'm doing all right."

He told me that when I got to New York, he would have his manager give me some money. He asked me to come to his hotel and have a little champagne and hors d'oeuvres. At that time Duke had cancer. When I entered his room, the whole place smelled like medicine. Because of his state of health, he wasn't allowed to drink. So he told me to have a drink of champagne with his manager. Duke and I talked for awhile. When he got back to New York, he died.

My next great loss came in 1981 with the death of Joe Louis in Las Vegas. Despite my sadness over his passing, I had seen Joe's demise coming for a long time. Joe's association with Las Vegas began in 1955, when he worked as a host at a white-owned place, the Moulin Rouge Hotel. In 1966 Joe and his third wife, Martha Malone Jefferson, moved from Los Angeles to Las Vegas, where Joe took a job in the public relations department of the Thunderbird Casino. The following year, he resigned and took a job as a greeter at Caesar's Palace. At this time he often came to see me, and I went out there to visit him. His health had worsened. His mind began to deteriorate from blows he had suffered in the ring. Although New York played a part, I believe Las Vegas was Joe's downfall. They say in Vegas that he was doing cocaine. I never saw him take drugs. If he was involved in them while I visited, I will never know. He never did them in front of me.

Joe's behind-the-scenes activities recall the time I went to see my old friend Ray Charles in Atlantic City. When I went to the stage door, I told the managers to alert Mr. Charles that his old landlord wanted to see him. One of the stage managers came and said that Mr. Charles was busy dressing and would see me after

172

the show. Thinking Mr. Charles was avoiding me, I became very peeved. I learned later, however, that he had a heroin addiction. Similar to Joe, Mr. Charles respected me and didn't want to expose his darker side. I am very fortunate that many of the entertainers never let me see this behavior because I may have thought differently of them. Despite Joe's drug problem, few people in Vegas looked out for his well-being like his friends and associates in Detroit and Chicago, who treated him as a friend, not as a celebrity.

But the owners of Caesar's Palace kept Joe busy. They made him a host, like the owners of the Desert Inn did for Joe's former opponent Billy Conn. Some think Joe's presence was purely honorary, without any importance, but he helped Caesar's Palace start the prizefights, which brought in millions of dollars. Joe made decent money in Las Vegas. Joe's wife Martha, a criminal lawyer, sat on Caesar's Palace's board of directors.

Several years before Joe took the job at Caesar's Palace, he wanted to open a hotel in Las Vegas and invited me to come out there. The backers, whom I do not wish to name, were bondsmen who operated businesses in Detroit and Las Vegas. The father of these young backers was my friend. In Las Vegas this man took me out to lunch to assess the proposition. He told me they wanted to put the hotel behind the Iron Curtain, my name for the black section of town. The idea of a family I had admired using the name of Joe Louis to open a club in a slum area disgusted me.

When I got back I told Joe not to let them open the club. If they had planned to open the hotel on the main strip, I could have agreed, but they insisted that Joe be confined to the black section of town. This I could not condone. I tried to talk Joe out of the idea, pointing out that not many blacks went to Las Vegas and that whites would not come to a club off in the black section. But Joe was hardheaded and determined. The backers got together and gave Joe the hotel. It wasn't a big place, just a hotel with a cabaret license.

Though Joe and his partners invited me to manage the hotel, I backed out by telling them I needed more money. They would not listen to my warning that Las Vegas, because of its racist policies in the hotels and casinos, would not attract enough black folks to support such a club. Six months later, the club folded and the backers lost all of their investment.

This wasn't the first time Joe followed the advice of people who sought to use his name. After Joe got out of the army, Jack Dempsey wanted to build a bar in Harlem for Joe. That I opposed also. At that time Jack Dempsey's corporation had bought Joe's contract. An individual can purchase the contract of a boxer just as they can an entertainer. You can buy it outright or on percentage. Jack Dempsey scheduled Joe to fight exhibition bouts and referee wrestling tournaments in New York and large cities in the New England states. Though Jack Dempsey had his own representatives, I stayed on to look after Joe's interests personally. After these contests we counted the money every night and sent most of it back to Mike Jacobs and Jack Dempsey's organization in New York.

In 1945 Jack Dempsey and his associates came up with the idea to build Joe a nightclub. Joe called me to come to his training camp at Pompton Lakes. I took a plane to New York City and then traveled to the camp by cab. At the camp Joe explained that Jack Dempsey had a site picked out for his cabaret on 125th Street in Harlem and that the architectural drawings had been completed. Despite the scarcity of steel at that time, he told me that Jack Dempsey had already purchased all the building materials. Though he wanted me to manage the club, I informed him that I refused to be associated with the establishment. With Joe's name and international prestige, he deserved a place on Forty-second Street or Broadway, not in a poor, black neighborhood. I viewed these offers, despite the backers' intentions, as prejudiced. I wanted Joe to go where the money was, where he could earn a respectable living. When I had my clubs, white people would come in and ask me, "Do you serve whites?" and I would answer, "Is this the United States of America?" I never turned away customers on account of their color and I would not allow Joe to submit to the prejudices of others. But Jack Dempsey went ahead and opened the place, the Joe Louis Bar, in 1946. When it closed not long after, it incurred a loss of ten thousand dollars.

In his last years Joe remained my first and foremost concern.

I didn't like people to take advantage of his good nature, especially after all he had done for others. On April 17, 1981, I attended his funeral service at Caesar's Palace Sports Pavilion in Las Vegas. In attendance were "The Rat Pack"—Frank Sinatra, Sammy Davis Jr., and Dean Martin—the Cotton Club Girls, and a host of other celebrities. Frank Sinatra and Sammy Davis said some laudatory words about Joe. Jesse Jackson delivered the sermon. Joe's body was interned in Arlington Cemetery. At that time, Arlington did not allow special burials, only those of deceased combat veterans. But by special permission from President Reagan, Joe was buried at Arlington. Though I was not present for the final service, I will forever be with Joe in spirit—in the memories he left not only for me but for millions of others.

As our old friend Leonard Reed once said, "Joe was a producer, not a consumer." It is still my contention that it is the responsibility of those in the position of leadership to help those less fortunate find jobs and education. If a community leader or politician seeks to better himself solely for the sake of making himself a name or filling his own pockets, he is not a true leader. Joe never separated himself from the people on the street, and neither did the majority of my Paradise Valley associates. They gave back to those who helped them.

Though most of these individuals are gone now, I have tried to carry on their fight. Throughout the 1980s I struggled to keep my nightclub open downtown. But with the closing of the Book Cadillac and the emptying of office buildings, my business could not survive. By late in the summer of 1987, the Celebrity Room was on its last legs. When the power company turned my lights off, I set up a makeshift bar outside on the sidewalk. I kept one waitress who doubled as a bartender. She worked four tables by candlelight and made change out of a cigar box. Even the restrooms had candles. With one service person I was still able to bring in a couple hundred dollars a night.

The newspapers printed stories about the financial state of my bar. I responded by informing the press that I wasn't giving up, "just retreating." I told readers, "Never tell 'em you're broke," adding that "In my era if you were broke, they would help you." Later that year, I closed the Celebrity Room.

Over the last two decades I have lived by the motto "Never retire." As a public relations consultant I have worked on numerous political campaigns and appeared as a guest speaker for a number of youth groups. In May 1993 the Urban League honored me as a Distinguished Warrior. For several years afterward, the Urban League has invited me, as part of their Distinguished Warrior award celebration, to talk before a group of black vocational students. After one of my talks, a six-foot-tall high-school student came out of the crowd and hugged me. He was so moved by my talk, he lifted me off the ground. This young man's enthusiasm demonstrated to me the importance of giving back to the young people—not just in monetary programs and paper promises, but in the sharing of our experiences, hardships, and insight they need in learning their history and building a future path of progress.

I have been fortunate that Detroiters continue to recognize my contributions. In July 1995 Mr. O'Neal Swanson, Dr. William Pickard, and Mr. Herbert Strather threw me a belated birthday celebration at Lenox Park on Detroit's riverfront. Surrounded by hundreds of old friends, I shook hands for hours, thanking the people who turned out to drink champagne and dine with their longtime friend, Mr. Sunnie Wilson. The music was provided by my close friend, Michigan Court of Appeals Judge Myron Wahls, and his trio. A fine judge, scholar, journalist, and musician, Myron Wahls is my "adoptive son." I was especially honored by a guest appearance by Detroit Mayor Dennis Archer who thanked me for my years of service to the community. I first met Mayor Archer when we worked on Mayor Young's first mayoral campaign.

Though I did not intend to make a speech that afternoon, I addressed the gathering with a few words concerning the future of our young people. "So ladies and gentlemen, they call me a legend. Maybe I am," I told the audience. "They say I've done so much. Maybe I have." After thanking my guests, however, I asked them to them to deliver one message to our young folks: "Go into business! I know you can be a lawyer or a doctor. Henry Ford was not a doctor. General Motors' president is not a doctor. Go into business!" I told the judges, "Before you sentence these peo-

176

ple to life in prison, think about your life and the struggle of the early black judges and attorneys who paved the way for your careers."

Next, I turned my attention to the children. I told the audience, "Mothers and fathers, I got a message for you. Stop letting money become the means of neglecting your kids. They need you. They need you in their infancy. They need you to encourage them. They want to go home to you and talk over their problems." I explained to the audience, "I was a wayward boy one time. . . . We had gangs—I'm from South Carolina. We had some mean gangs. Bad gangs." Then I made reference to the gentlemen down South, the Cooper brothers, who helped and encouraged me to pursue a positive path in life. "We must remember that there is more to this life than material gain. Because if the home life is not there, we have lost our foundation. With the craving for material wealth, few people have time for the children and no time to show them love or affection."

In my final words I served up a verbal toast to all those who had helped me down through the years, the whites and the blacks—all the individuals who saw the potential in Sunnie Wilson and allowed him to get a chance in life. To those in attendance and the countless others who have touched my life, I give my thanks.

◆ 9 ◆
Lucky Old Fella

On September 8, 1987, I was honored at a golden anniversary celebration at the Latin Quarter on East Grand Boulevard. A combination seventy-ninth birthday and celebratory tribute, the event drew hundreds of people, including Mayor Coleman Young, Judge Myron Wahls, and Dennis Archer, then a Michigan Supreme Court justice. Acting as the honorary emcee, Mayor Young took the stage and announced: "I'm certainly glad to be here with all of you who are obviously are Sunnie Wilson's friends, to help celebrate his . . . birthday. There are some of you out there who might question whether the count is accurate. . . . For those of you who have attended some of Sunnie's birthday parties, you know he's already had eight hundred."

Under the direction of Dr. Thomas Beans Bowles, the house band included another Motown great, pianist Earl Van Dyke. The featured performers were Arthur Prysock, Jan Spencer, the tap dance team the Sultans, the Paradise Valley Dancers, Lottie the Body, Motown singer Kim Weston, blues vocalist Alberta Adams, and singer Nellie Hill of Flame Show Bar fame. Dancer Flash Beaver did a routine dedicated to the Forest Club roller rink skaters. He thanked me for giving him his first job at the Forest Club. Flash went on to Broadway and even appeared on the *Ed Sullivan Show.*

One of the highlights of the party was a guest appearance by my former hotel guest, B. B. King. When B. B. was asked to play

179

at my party, he refused to accept any money for his appearance. He flew into town from New York on his way to New Orleans. He came to the party without his guitar, Lucille. When he got on stage he planned on just singing. The mayor humorously told the crowd that he heard that B. B. "was going to dance." Addressing the crowd, B. B. recounted our first meeting when he came to town with his band. "When I first came to Detroit, we ran out of money on our way here," he said. "Somebody told me about a hotel where I could talk to a gentleman. . . . I'm speaking of Mr. Wilson. From that time on I have been grateful." B. B. began to sing and in the middle of his performance, he borrowed the rhythm guitarist's instrument and broke into his 1970 hit, "The Thrill Is Gone." B. B.'s tribute to me proved the value of friendship and the respect received from helping a friend.

In my years in Detroit, people have been very kind in offering me positions that would have put me comfortably behind a desk. I'm not a desk man. John Dancy of the Urban League wanted me to work for him; others invited me to run for political office. During World War II, the army offered me a non-commissioned officer's rank to run the mess hall at Selfridge Air Base. As an independent and business-minded individual, I just couldn't, after years of establishing myself as a promoter and entrepreneur, work under someone, no matter how much money the job offered. I wanted to remain close with the people on the street, to promote my acts, and to watch talented young people pursue their careers. Some didn't make it and others later became stars or successful politicians. Down through the years, my reward for helping young entertainers, politicians, and the like has been watching their progress. I have had the opportunity to observe these young talents grow.

I kept company with many talented people. Back in the forties, I courted Savannah Churchill, who appeared with the Benny Carter Orchestra. She wasn't just nice looking, she was beautiful. Her picture often appeared on the covers of black magazines. Although Savannah Churchill built quite a name for herself, she never did become as big as Ella Fitzgerald or Dinah Washington. But I knew a number of talented people who were great, but never reached stardom—individuals who strived to make a name for themselves in the years when segregation limited their opportunities.

Along with the judges, black businessmen like me thought desegregation would open up a new era. When they introduced integration in the mid-1950s, I thought it was going to be a two-way street for blacks and whites. Black businessmen thought it would strengthen the economic condition of our community. After integration, however, the white people didn't have to go downtown to blind pigs and after-hours spots for entertainment. Instead, they drew the black entertainers into their clubs and lounges. The whites stopped spending money in the black neighborhoods. Although I fought for integration all my life, I never thought it would become a one-way street.

Total integration is not in the scheme of things. It's not meant to be. You have to face the facts. You've got to deal with prejudice. If blacks choose to ignore it, they will never overcome it. Turn the corner and old Jim Crow will always be there. But the young people must know the facts so that they realize there are bad white people and bad black people.

Black people are not yet equal and they will not be equal until they improve their economic condition. The only major thing that separates blacks from whites is that black folks don't have as much money. Many of us have lost the spirit of accomplishment. Black folks must stop being consumers and become producers. Though many have business on their mind, they must learn to become business minded. Back in earlier days we had to carve out our place by establishing private businesses—hotels, nightclubs, insurance companies, and the like. If Duke Ellington were alive today, I would tell him to turn the A Train around and send it across the country to announce, borrowing my old friend Louis Jordan's message, "Open the Door Richard" and let these young people in. Let these young, qualified students, doctors, and lawyers in the mainstream.

This brings to mind a tale I heard as a child down in South Carolina, a story pertaining to a black fella named Ben who was confined to a colored mental institution. On Sunday, as the story went, a white inspector came by with the preacher to check on the patients. The inspector greeted Ben with, "How you doin', Ben?"

Just then, Ben began walking toward the inspector. Frightened by Ben's approach, the inspector started to move faster toward his car. As the inspector picked up his pace Ben started to trot after him, causing the white man to stumble to the ground in terror. Standing over him, Ben lightly touched the man, shouting "Tag!"

This is my point—black folks need to catch up and it does no good for the white man to run, because we're coming anyway. We harbor no malice. We just want opportunity.

Over sixty years ago in South Carolina, I saw something in a local white newspaper, *The Grit,* that also made a lasting impression on my mind. In this paper I saw series of pictures of a black man. The first one showed him in slavery, chained and reading the Bible. The second portrayed him free from his shackles, attending school. Next, he sat in Congress during Reconstruction, and in the last picture he was campaigning for the presidency. Looking at this newspaper page, I could feel the struggle of my forebears, what they had, and what we still must do to forge ahead.

Today the black man and the white man both suffer from their own respective complexes. Many young black folks have fallen into the self-fulfilling prophecy of disbelief—that they cannot make a mark in the world around them, that education is something the white man has forced upon them. Many white liberals in America, on the other hand, have been feeling guilt over past acts, of the injustices of slavery, peonage, and segregation.

In this continuing path of progress one thing is paramount—the importance of education, of being prepared to enter the realm of business and politics. If you are prepared, if you have the proper educational background and are qualified to fill a position, they will find you. Different classes will always exist, regardless of color or ethnicity—that you cannot escape—but you can escape economic dependence by getting an education. I once endeavored to become an entertainer and discovered that I did not have enough talent to fulfill my dream. This did not hinder me from continuing my search for a direction in life. My true talent was business and public relations. In other words, the secret to success is persistence and perseverance, of finding and nurturing one's true talent.

I was a wayward boy once and I tried to do my best to learn from others, to seek the company of good people, irrespective of color and creed. In my lifetime I never had many problems of being denied this or that, because I always fought for progress. I have had a good life, because I have met good people. I would not trade it for another life. Maybe I've been a lucky old fella.

Sources

Primary

"Ace Showman Says Top Line Hard to Find." *Michigan Chronicle,* September 3, 1949, p. 21.

Adams, Alberta. Telephone interview with the author. Detroit, February 27, 1997.

Adams, Gus. Telephone interview with the author. Detroit, January 28, 1997. Personal interview with the author. Detroit, February 1, 1997.

"Advice of FBI Asked in Quiz." *Detroit News,* August 23, 1939, p. 1.

Ashby, John. "Idlewild: She's Black, She's Beautiful, She's the Aging Red Hot Mamma of Michigan's Resorts." *Detroit Free Press,* August 16, 1970, p. 7.

Bevier, Thomas. "Idlewild Shakes Free of Past." *Detroit News,* March 3, 1991, p. 7.

"Bits and Pieces." *Michigan Chronicle,* March 4, 1989, sec. C, p. 4.

Bohy, Ric. "Paradise Laid to Rest: Nightclubs Are Gone, But Idlewild Thrives." *Detroit News,* August 19, 1985, sec. A, p. 9.

Boykin, Ulysses. "Bulletin Board." *Detroit Tribune,* July 10, 1937.

——— . "Jumpin' Jive." *Detroit Tribune,* February 15, 1941, p. 10; March 1, 1941, p. 8.

"Bulletin Board." *Detroit Tribune,* October 23, 1937, p. 9.

Carlisle, John M. "Grand Jury Petition Made to Court: Judges Called to Act Monday." *Detroit News,* August 19, 1939, p. 1.

——— . "I'm Just a Small-Time Guy, McBride Insists to Police." *Detroit News,* August 8, 1939, pp. 1–2.

Chandler, Paul. "Brown Bomber Hits the Road for 5:30 A.M. Gallop." *Detroit News,* April 22, 1951.

"Charges Dropped by Police: Mayor's Name Enters Hearing." *Detroit News,* November 13, 1939, p. 1.

"Colossal Chronicle Exposition Ends with 25,000 Gate Total and Memories of Prizes Galore." *Michigan Chronicle,* June 3, 1950, p. 1.

"Come to Beautiful Idlewild for a Real Vacation." Pamphlet published by the Idlewild Chamber of Commerce, Idlewild, August 3, 1953.

"Comparison of Fight Camps Favors Joe's Spirit." *Detroit News,* May 21, 1946.

Conot, Robert. *American Odyssey.* New York: William Morrow, 1974.

Cowans, Russell. "Broadway Joe Passes from Scene." *Michigan Chronicle,* August 6, 1960, p. 7.

Cozy Corner advertisement. "Now Open." *Michigan Chronicle,* May 6, 1933, p. 2.

Craig, Charlotte. "Sunnie Wilson: Entertainer Keeps Song in His Heart." *Detroit Free Press,* August 23, 1987, p. 3.

Dawson, Jim. Liner notes to the album *Hadda Brooks: That's My Desire.* Virgin Records 39687 2. 1994.

Deramus, Betty. "Detroit's 'Unofficial Black History' Unfolded in Classy Quarters." *Detroit News,* January 31, 1993, sec. C, p. 6.

"Detroit Turns Out for a Great Guy!" *Courier,* October 24, 1953.

"Detroit Urban League Honors Six Distinguished Warriors." *Detroit Free Press,* March 17, 1993, pp. 1–2.

"Diggs Given 50-50 Chance." *Michigan Chronicle,* January 13, 1951, p. 1.

"Dual Slaying Recalls Case of Robinson." *Detroit News,* August 7, 1939, p. 1.

Duncan, Francis. "The Story of the D & C." *Inland Seas,* 1953, pp. 49–55.

"Everybody's Got a Haven." *Michigan Chronicle,* June 16, 1951, p. 13.

Ford, Rikki. "City's Clubs, Idlewild Produced World-Class Talent in the 50's." *Michigan Chronicle,* September 27, 1986, sec. E, p. 17.

"Forest Club Ballroom" (advertisement). *Michigan Chronicle,* June 19, 1943, p. 18.

"Fugitive from Grand Jury Starts Extradition Fight." *Detroit News,* February 10, 1940, p. 1.

"G. T. Roumell Dies; Built Catering Empire." *Detroit News,* June 1969, obituary section.

Gilchrist, Brenda J. "Detroit's 1943 Race Riot, 50 Years Ago Today, Still Seems Too Soon." *Detroit Free Press,* June 20, 1993, p. 5.

Graham, Isola. Telephone interview with the author. Detroit, July 31, 1996.

"Grand Jury Pleas: 2nd Petition Submitted by Council." *Detroit News,* August 21, 1939, p. 1.

Harris, Russell. "Crowds Still Wild about Harry but Turnout Is Below Estimate." *Detroit News,* October 31, 1952.

Holsey, Steve. "Dignitaries, Stars at Sunnie Wilson's Bash." *Michigan Chronicle,* September 19, 1987, sec. C, p. 1.

"Idlewild Social Notes." *Michigan Chronicle,* August 13, 1949, p. 19.

Jackson, Kathy. "Sunnie Rising Again? Benefit Will Aid Innkeeper Who Brought Stars to Detroit." *Crain's Detroit Business,* August 17, 1987, pp. 1, 28.

"Joe Louis: How He Taught a Generation." *Detroit Free Press,* April 13, 1981, p. 3.

"John White Tells Story of Raid: T-Men Hit Gotham Hotel Like Raging Football Team; Hammer and Axes Used by Agents to Smash Doors." *Michigan Chronicle,* November 17, 1962, pp. 1–4.

Johnson, Ziggy. "Zaggin' with Ziggy." *Michigan Chronicle,* October 27, 1951, p. 19; May 31, 1952, p. 19; August 11, 1962, p. 2.

Jones, Isaac. "Hastings after Dark." *Michigan Chronicle,* August 6, 1949, p. 23.

"Jumpin' with Jive." *Michigan Chronicle,* June 14, 1941, p. 11.

Kotolowitz, Alex. "Idle Awhile in Idlewild." *Detroit News,* May 6, 1984, p. 16.

Lane, Bill. "Former Cozy Corner Owner Mac Ivey Recalls His Early Days in Detroit." *Michigan Chronicle,* August 27, 1949, p. 21.

———. "Strong Pleas Made by Both CIO and AFL." *Detroit Tribune,* April 5, 1941, p. 1.

———. "Swinging Down the Lane." *Michigan Chronicle,* December 16, 1950, p. 24; February 3, 1951, p. 21; September 1, 1951, p. 10; January 5, 1952, p. 10.

Lawson, Hugh. Telephone interview with author. White Plains, New York, March 27, 1996.

"Legion Plans to Ignore Paul Robeson Concert." *Michigan Chronicle,* October 1, 1949, p. 7.

"Leo Adler Dies; Prominent Auto Dealer, Zionist." *Jewish News*, June 4, 1965.

"Line-up New Starline Friday at Sunnie Wilson's." *Michigan Chronicle*, June 10, 1950, p. 21.

McConnell, Darci. "Federal Attention and Money Give a Michigan Region and Its People a Needed Boost and Put a . . . County on the Move." *Detroit Free Press*, December 10, 1996, sec. A, pp. 1, 9.

"McGrath to Talk for State." *Detroit News*, January 6, 1941, p. 1.

McLeod, Jackie. Telephone interview with author. Detroit, March 20, 1996.

"Mother Kills Girl and Self: Shattered Romance With Gambler Leads Woman to Make Accusations Before Ending 2 Lives in Auto." *Detroit News*, August 7, 1939, pp. 1–2.

"Negro Hotelman White Dies at 55." *Detroit Free Press*, July 9, 1964.

"New Police Superintendent Is Smart, Tough and Fair." *Detroit News*, October 10, 1945.

Noble, William T. "Made a Million Buying Businesses Strange to Him." *Detroit News*, August 30, 1958.

"One of the Finest Black Resorts, Surf Club in Land Dispute." *Windsor Star*, April 18, 1979.

"Operators Motivated by Inquiry." *Detroit News*, August 1939, p. 1.

"Order Snub for Robeson." *Detroit News*, September 25, 1949, p. 3.

"Paul Robeson Scheduled to Sing and Speak Here." *Detroit Tribune*, September 24, 1949, p. 7.

Phillips, Ron. "Turnabout: Sunnie Wilson at Latin Quarter." *Michigan Chronicle*, September 5, 1987, sec. B, p. 1.

"Police Praised by Robeson." *Michigan Chronicle*, October 10, 1949, p. 11.

"Popular Show Boss Bows Out." *Michigan Chronicle*, January 20, 1951, p. 20.

"President Truman to Speak Here Thursday." *Michigan Chronicle*, November 1, 1952.

"Reading Gets 4 to 5 Years for Graft." *Detroit News*, January 7, 1942, p. 1.

"Reading Plans Graft Appeal." *Detroit News*, January 8, 1942, p. 5.

"Revival Is in the Wings for Idlewild." *Detroit News,* March 27, 1988, pp. 1, 2.

"Robeson Riot Quiz Ordered." *Detroit News,* September 25, 1949, p. 3.

Scott, Nathaniel. "Sunnie Wilson: Keeping Dollars in the Community." *Michigan Citizen,* February 26–March 3, 1992, sec. A, p. 6.

Seymour, Frank M. "See More with Seymour, More about Idlewild." *Michigan Chronicle,* June 21, 1952, p. 21.

"Sketches of a Non-Incumbent." *Detroit News,* February 17, 1953, p. 24.

"The Spectator." *Michigan Chronicle,* October 8, 1949, p. 22.

Stewart, Betty. "When Darkness Falls." *Michigan Chronicle,* December 8, 1951, p. 21; October 1952, p. 7.

"Stutz Anderson Reflects on Fledging Days." *Michigan Chronicle,* March 7, 1964.

"Sunnie Wilson to File Suit Against Attorney Samuel Rubin for Forest Club Enterprise." *Michigan Chronicle,* November 25, 1950.

"Sunnie Wilson Sells Forest Club For $40,000." *Michigan Chronicle,* November 18, 1950, pp. 1, 4.

"Surf Club Members Get Holiday Spirit." *Michigan Chronicle,* November 10, 1951, p. 15.

Sweeny, Anne. "The Sunnie Side of the Street." *Detroit Free Press,* September 6, 1987.

"They Deserve Confidence." *Detroit News,* August 22, 1939, p. 1.

"Travelers Hotel Directory" (advertisement). *The Crisis,* September 7, 1938.

"U.S. Adds Rackets to Quiz List." *Detroit News,* October 24, 1939, p. 1.

Vest, Rollo. *Detroit Tribune,* August 18, 1934, p. 5.

Weist, Jan. "Little Ghost Town Starts to Rebuild." *Detroit News,* March 6, 1980, p. 4.

"We'll Just Call You Joe Louis." *Detroit Free Press,* April 13, 1981, p. 12.

Wowk, Mike. "6 Honored as Civil Rights Warriors." *Detroit News,* March 18, 1993.

"Youngsters Rollick at Christmas Party." *Michigan Chronicle,* January 1, 1949, p. 19.

Additional information concerning Springhill Farm provided in a private meeting with the members of the Shelby Historical Committee, Shelby Township Building, Utica, Michigan, April 1996.

VHS Video Tape of Sunnie Wilson's seventy-ninth birthday celebration at the Latin Quarter, Detroit, 1987. Excerpts of dialogue were quoted from the speakers and guests present at the event.

Secondary

Allen University Handbook, 1994–1995.

Armbruster, Ann. *The Life and Times of Miami Beach.* New York: Knopf, 1995.

Bak, Richard. *Joe Louis: The Great Black Hope.* Dallas: Taylor Publishing, 1996.

Barrow, Joe Louis Jr., with Barbara Munder. *Joe Louis: 50 Years an American Hero.* New York: McGraw-Hill, 1988.

Boris, Joseph J., ed. *Who's Who of Colored America: A Biographical Dictionary of Notable Persons of African Descent in America, 1928–29.* 2d ed. New York: Who's Who in Colored America Corp., 1929.

Brown, Tindall George. *South Carolina Negroes, 1877–1900.* Baton Rouge: Louisiana State University Press, 1966.

Cantor, George. *Historic Landmarks of Black America.* Detroit: Gale Research, 1990.

Chilton, John, with foreword by Johnny Simmen. *Who's Who of Jazz: Storyville to Swing.* Philadelphia: Chilton Book Company, 1978.

Chilton, John. *McKinney's Music: A Bio-Discography of McKinney's Cotton Pickers.* London: Bloomsbury Bookshop, 1978.

City Directory of Columbia South Carolina, 1927. Columbia: The State Co. Printer and Pub., 1927.

"Cleanest Champion, Sorry Investor." *Ebony Magazine* (May 1946).

Cohassey, John. "Down on Hastings Street: A Study of Social and Cultural Changes in a Detroit Community, 1941–1955." Master's thesis, Wayne State University, 1993.

Collins, Nigel. *Boxing Babylon: Behind the Shadowy World of the Prize Ring.* New York: Citadel Press, 1990.

Dance, Helen Oakley. *Stormy Monday: The T-Bone Walker Story.* New York: Da Capo, 1987.

Devlin, George A. *South Carolina and the Black Migration, 1865–1940: In Search of the Promiseland.* New York: Garland, 1989.

Duberman, Martin B. *Paul Robeson.* New York: Knopf, 1988.

Dunning, John. *Tune in Yesterday: The Ultimate Encyclopedia of Old Time Radio, 1925–1976.* Englewood Cliffs, N.J.: Prentice-Hall, 1976.

Foner, Philip S., ed. *Paul Robeson Speaks: Writings, Speeches, Interviews, 1918–1974.* New York: Citadel Press, 1978.

Gilliam, Dorothy Butler. *Paul Robeson: All American.* Washington, D.C.: New Republic Books, 1978.

Good Morning Blues: The Autobiography of Count Basie. As told to Albert Murray. New York: Da Capo, 1985.

Gordon, Asa H. *Sketches of Negro Life in South Carolina.* 2d ed. Columbia: University of South Carolina Press, 1929.

Gourse, Leslie. *Unforgettable: The Life and Mystique of Nat King Cole.* New York: St. Martin's Press, 1991.

Hampton, Lionel, with James Haskins. *Hamp: An Autobiography.* New York: Warner Books, 1989.

Hemmingway, Theodore. "Prelude to Change: Black Carolinians in the War Years, 1914–1920." *Journal of Negro History* 65, no. 3 (summer 1980).

Henderson, Wilma Wood. *Detroit Perspectives: Crossroads and Turning Points.* Detroit: Wayne State University Press, 1991.

Henry, Robert Selph. *The Story of Reconstruction.* New York: Bobbs-Merrill, 1938.

History of the Class of 1910, University of South Carolina. Published by the 1910 Class History Committee, 1961.

Hollis, R. Lynch. *The Black Urban Condition: A Documentary History, 1860–1971.* New York: Thomas Y. Crowell Book Company, 1973.

Jacoway, Elizabeth, and David R. Colburn, eds. *Southern Businessmen and Segregation.* Baton Rouge: Louisiana State University Press, 1982.

Johnson, Elmer D., and Kathleen Lewis Sloan, eds. *South Carolina: A Documentary Profile of the Palmetto State.* Columbia: University of South Carolina Press, 1971.

Keller, Francis Richardson. *An American Crusade: The Life of Charles Waddell Chesnutt.* Provo, Utah: Brigham Young University Press, 1978.

Lake County: A Collection of Historical Writings Compiled by the Lake County Historical Society. M&M Printing and Graphics, 1994.

Libby, Bill. *Joe Louis: The Brown Bomber.* New York: Lothrop, Lee, and Shepard Books, 1980.

Louis, Joe. *The Joe Louis Story.* New York: Grosset and Dunlop, 1953.

Louis, Joe, with Edna and Art Rust, Jr. *Joe Louis: My Life.* New York: Harcourt Brace Jovanovich, 1978.

Maltin, Leonard, and Richard W. Bann. *The Little Rascals: The Life and Times of Our Gang.* New enlarged, updated edition. New York: Crown Trade Paperbacks, 1992.

McGhee, Scott, and Susan Watson, eds. *Blacks in Detroit: A Reprint of Articles from the Detroit Free Press.* Detroit: Detroit Free Press, 1980.

Mead, Chris. *Champion Joe Louis: Black Hero in White America.* London: Robson Books, 1986.

Meier, August, and Elliott Rudwick. *Black Detroit and the Rise of the UAW.* New York: Oxford University Press, 1979.

Michigan Ghost Towns Vol. II. N.p.: Royal Dodge, 1971.

Michigan Places and Names: The History of the Founding and the Naming of More Than Five Thousand Past and Present Michigan Communities. Detroit: Wayne State University Press, 1973.

Moon, Elaine Latzman. *Untold Tales, Unsung Heroes: An Oral History of Detroit's African American Community, 1918–1967.* Detroit: Wayne State University Press, 1994.

Nevins, Allan, and Frank Ernest Hill. *Ford, Decline and Rebirth, 1933–1962.* New York: Charles Scribner's Sons, 1962.

Newby, I. A. *Black Carolinians: A History of Blacks in South Carolina from 1895 to 1968.* Columbia: University of South Carolina Press, 1973.

Perry, Charlotte, ed. *The Official Business and Professional Guide of Detroit, 1947.* 7th ed. Detroit: Charlotte Perry, Pub., 1947.

Polk's Detroit City Directory. Detroit: Polk and Company, 1922.

Polk's Detroit Directory 1936. Detroit: L. Polk, 1936.

Robinson, Sugar Ray, with Dave Anderson. *Sugar Ray: The Sugar Ray Robinson Story.* New York: Da Capo, 1969.

Sterling, Alfred. *The Man from Missouri: The Life and Times of Harry S Truman.* New York: G. P. Putman's Sons, 1962.

Taylor, Alrutheus Ambush. *The Negro in South Carolina during Reconstruction.* New York: Russell and Russell, 1969.

Thomas, Richard W. *Life Is What We Make It: Building a Black Community in Detroit, 1915–1945.* Bloomington: Indiana University Press, 1992.

Travis, Dempsey J. *An Autobiography of Black Jazz.* With an introduction by Studs Terkel. Chicago: Urban Research Institute, 1983.

Wen, Pehyun. "Idlewild—A Negro Village in Lake County, Michigan." Master's thesis, University of Chicago, 1972.

Williamson, Joel. *After Slavery: The Negro in South Carolina during Reconstruction, 1861–1877.* Chapel Hill: University of North Carolina Press, 1965.

Wolff, Daniel, with S. R. Crain, Clifton White, and G. David Tenenbaum. *You Send Me: The Life and Times of Sam Cooke.* New York: Quill William Morrow, 1995.

Young, Coleman, with Lonnie Wheeler. *Hard Stuff: The Autobiography of Mayor Coleman Young.* New York: Viking, 1994.

Additional information on the historical background of Allen University was acquired from sources compiled by the U.S. Department of the Interior, located in the South Carolina Archives and History.

Index

TITLES IN THE GREAT LAKES BOOKS SERIES

Wolf in Sheep's Clothing: The Search for a Child Killer, by Tommy McIntyre, 1988

Copper-Toed Boots, by Marguerite de Angeli, 1989 (reprint)

Detroit Images: Photographs of the Renaissance City, edited by John J. Bukowczyk and Douglas Aikenhead, with Peter Slavcheff, 1989

Hangdog Reef: Poems Sailing the Great Lakes, by Stephen Tudor, 1989

Detroit: City of Race and Class Violence, revised edition, by B. J. Widick, 1989

Deep Woods Frontier: A History of Logging in Northern Michigan, by Theodore J. Karamanski, 1989

Orvie, The Dictator of Dearborn, by David L. Good, 1989

Seasons of Grace: A History of the Catholic Archdiocese of Detroit, by Leslie Woodcock Tentler, 1990

The Pottery of John Foster: Form and Meaning, by Gordon and Elizabeth Orear, 1990

The Diary of Bishop Frederic Baraga: First Bishop of Marquette, Michigan, edited by Regis M. Walling and Rev. N. Daniel Rupp, 1990

Walnut Pickles and Watermelon Cake: A Century of Michigan Cooking, by Larry B. Massie and Priscilla Massie, 1990

The Making of Michigan, 1820–1860: A Pioneer Anthology, edited by Justin L. Kestenbaum, 1990

America's Favorite Homes: A Guide to Popular Early Twentieth-Century Homes, by Robert Schweitzer and Michael W. R. Davis, 1990

Beyond the Model T: The Other Ventures of Henry Ford, by Ford R. Bryan, 1990

Life after the Line, by Josie Kearns, 1990

Michigan Lumbertowns: Lumbermen and Laborers in Saginaw, Bay City, and Muskegon, 1870–1905, by Jeremy W. Kilar, 1990

Detroit Kids Catalog: The Hometown Tourist by Ellyce Field, 1990

Charting the Inland Seas: A History of the U.S. Lake Survey, by Arthur M. Woodford, 1994 (reprint)

Ojibwa Narratives of Charles and Charlotte Kawbawgam and Jacques LePique, 1893–1895. Recorded with Notes by Homer H. Kidder, edited by Arthur P. Bourgeois, 1994, co-published with the Marquette County Historical Society

Strangers and Sojourners: A History of Michigan's Keweenaw Peninsula, by Arthur W. Thurner, 1994

Win Some, Lose Some: G. Mennen Williams and the New Democrats, by Helen Washburn Berthelot, 1995

Sarkis, by Gordon and Elizabeth Orear, 1995

The Northern Lights: Lighthouses of the Upper Great Lakes, by Charles K. Hyde, 1995 (reprint)

Kids Catalog of Michigan Adventures, second edition, by Ellyce Field, 1995

Rumrunning and the Roaring Twenties: Prohibition on the Michigan-Ontario Waterway, by Philip P. Mason, 1995

In the Wilderness with the Red Indians, by E. R. Baierlein, translated by Anita Z. Boldt, edited by Harold W. Moll, 1996

Elmwood Endures: History of a Detroit Cemetery, by Michael Franck, 1996

Master of Precision: Henry M. Leland, by Mrs. Wilfred C. Leland with Minnie Dubbs Millbrook, 1996 (reprint)

Haul-Out: New and Selected Poems, by Stephen Tudor, 1996

Kids Catalog of Michigan Adventures, third edition, by Ellyce Field, 1997

Beyond the Model T: The Other Ventures of Henry Ford, by Ford R. Bryan, 1997 (reprint)

Young Henry Ford: A Picture History of the First Forty Years, by Sidney Olson, 1997 (reprint)

The Coast of Nowhere: Meditations on Rivers, Lakes, and Streams, by Michael Delp, 1997

The Long Winter Ends, by Newton G. Thomas, 1997 (reprint)

These Men Have Seen Hard Service: The First Michigan Sharpshooters in the Civil War, by Raymond J. Herek, 1997

From Saginaw Valley to Tin Pan Alley: Saginaw's Contribution to American Popular Music, 1890–1955, by R. Grant Smith, 1998

Toast of the Town: The Life and Times of Sunnie Wilson, by Sunnie Wilson with John Cohassey, 1998